CH00657283

# The Single woman's su

A wealth of information and advice for the woman who wants to make the most of her freedom.

*In the same series*

COMING LATE TO MOTHERHOOD
  Joan Michelson and Sue Gee
THE PREMENSTRUAL SYNDROME
  Caroline Shreeve
THE SECOND NINE MONTHS
  Judith Gansberg and Arthur Mostel
SEX DURING PREGNANCY AND AFTER CHILDBIRTH
  Sylvia Close
THE WORKING WOMAN'S GUIDE
  Liz Hodgkinson

# The Single woman's survival guide

An indispensable companion to the pleasures
and problems of an independent life

*by*

## Lee Rodwell

THORSONS PUBLISHERS LIMITED
Wellingborough, Northamptonshire

First published July 1985
Second Impression August 1985

© LEE RODWELL 1985

*This book is sold subject to the condition that it shall not, by way of trade or otherwise, be lent, re-sold, hired out, or otherwise circulated without the publisher's prior consent in any form of binding or cover other than that in which it is published and without a similar condition including this condition being imposed on the subsequent purchaser.*

British Library Cataloguing in Publication Data

Rodwell, Lee
    The single woman's survival guide: an indispensable guide
    to the pleasures and problems of an independent life.
    1. Single people    2. Single women — Conduct of life
    I. Title
    306.8'8    HQ799.2

    ISBN 0-7255-1105-1

Printed and bound in Great Britain by
Anchor Brendon Ltd, Tiptree, Essex

# Contents

| | Page |
|---|---|
| *Introduction* | 7 |
| *Chapter* | |
| 1. The Single Woman at Home | 17 |
| 2. The Single Woman at Work | 34 |
| 3. The Single Woman and Sex | 49 |
| 4. The Single Woman and Men | 70 |
| 5. The Single Woman and the Law | 85 |
| 6. The Single Woman at the Shops | 96 |
| 7. The Single Woman and her Money | 109 |
| 8. The Single Woman and Children | 124 |
| 9. The Single Woman on Holiday | 148 |
| 10. The Single Woman Staying Healthy | 159 |
| 11. The Single Woman Staying Safe | 176 |
| *Index* | 189 |

# Introduction

There are a lot of us about – more than three and a half million in the sixteen to forty age range alone. Single women: teenagers living at home; students at college; young girls going out to work and sharing flats; women in their thirties and forties, holding down careers, paying off their own mortgages, even having children or raising families on their own.

Being single no longer makes you the odd woman out. Being single is even, somehow, considered smart. Today the label implies glamour rather than the stigma of spinsterhood. For times have changed since writer Simone de Beauvoir asserted that marriage is traditionally the destiny offered to women by society: 'Most women are married or have been or plan to be or suffer from not being.'

These days women can shape their own destiny. Since the social and sexual upheavals of the 1960s, the ranks of single women have been swelling. More and more of us have found ourselves agreeing, not with de Beauvoir, but with that sixties' prophet and pacemaker Helen Gurley Brown who said:

> You may marry or you may not. In today's world that is no longer the question for women.
>
> Those who glom on to men so that they can collapse with relief, spend the rest of their days shining up their status symbol and figure they never have to reach, stretch, learn, grow, face dragons or make a living, are the ones to be pitied. They, in my opinion, are the unfulfilled ones.

Certainly the trend is for women to spend more of their adult life in the single state than they used to – not only are women tending to marry later, but many more of them return to singledom, if that is the right word, after divorce.

We have learnt the lesson that marriage is not the answer to everything. Getting married is no longer the only socially acceptable way for a girl to leave her parents' home and set up on her own. We no longer feel we have to marry for sex. In the fifties, 66 per cent of women said they had waited until their wedding night before making love to their man. By the seventies only 18 per cent of women had not already been to bed with the man they wed.

Even pregnancy is no longer a cast-iron reason for getting married. The single woman who finds herself pregnant today may equally choose abortion or single parenthood.

Nor do we feel we have to stay married for the security that marriage is supposed to provide. Two-thirds of divorce petitions are now filed by women. Better education, a wider choice of jobs and the knowledge that women can, if they want, support themselves, has given many the self confidence to start over again on their own.

Whether we all agreed with the feminist movement or not, some of the messages it preached hit home. We may not believe, as one of the slogans put it, that 'a woman without a man is like a fish without a bicycle'. But many of us saw the bitter truth in another: 'You start off by sinking into his arms, and end up with your arms in his sink'.

American research has shown that, for women, being single is good for you. Single women are the healthiest citizens of all, single men the unhealthiest. But marriage turns that male-female situation right on its head.

Of course, there is a danger of romanticizing the single state, of looking at it in the way we used to look at marriage through rose-tinted glasses. Being single is rarely a round of exciting parties, being wooed by droves of wildly attractive men, zooming off into the sunset in your own Porsche.

Being single can mean wrestling with your own tax returns, telling your boss in no uncertain terms that you do not fancy him, learning how to change a washer on a tap, getting up five times in the night because your child is ill and having to go to work next morning worrying whether the nursery will phone to say he is at death's door.

Being single can also mean very different things at different stages of our lives. It can be a positive choice, or something that simply creeps up on you.

*Barbara* is twenty-six, has no steady relationship at present and no great desire to 'settle down and get married'. She used to work as a store detective but is currently 'temping' and she shares a flat in London. She says:

> I left home when I was 19, much to my parents' horror and disbelief. They still thought I was a child. They were convinced I couldn't cope on my own, but I have, quite nicely, thank you.
>
> I suppose I would like, one day, to find that long-term, perfect relationship. I think, if they're honest, most single women eventually want to be part of a couple. But not necessarily right now.
>
> It's a cliché but it's true: when you are single you can do whatever you want, when you want. You don't have to think about Us – it's only I and Me. There's no one around to bring you down when you're flying high or trying to cheer you up when you are quite happy feeling miserable. You don't have to put on an act.
>
> Of course there are disadvantages. Maybe you go out with someone for a couple of dates and it doesn't work out. So you go out with another, and another. And sometimes it just seems so shallow. There are times when I'd rather sit at home and read a book than go through the motions again. But then I get bored with my own company and make a concerted effort. Despite what some women say, there are plenty of men out there.
>
> It's important to do things because you want to do them, not because you think you'll meet men that way. I belong to a club called the Dracula Society and they are a great bunch

of people. We watch films, have meetings, go on holidays to Rumania and generally have a good laugh.

I never feel I need a man around to look after me – I'm pretty used to looking after myself now. It's what I've got used to. What bugs me is what I call the Noah's Ark syndrome – where other couples assume everyone else has to be like them, going everywhere two by two. They see single women as a threat to their relationships.

But if I was part of a couple I'd make sure I kept in touch with my single friends. Otherwise a relationship tends to stagnate. I like being single. I want it to stay interesting. On the other hand I don't want to end up in the years to come, broke, bored and alone. But right now I'm not about to settle for second best. I certainly don't equate being single with being on the shelf!

*Jill* is thirty-eight, the head teacher of an inner city infants school, who owns a house jointly with another single, female teacher. Although she has had a number of long-term relationships she has never married.

She says:

I never thought I'd be single all my life. I always imagined that I'd get married in my mid-twenties and have a family. There was a time, when I was about twenty-five or so, when it worried me. But by the time I was in my late twenties I realized it wasn't going to happen *and it wasn't what I wanted anyway.*

I'd already bought the house. I think the nesting instinct tends to take over in your late twenties whether you are married or not. There's a growing feeling of not wanting to be at the mercy of a landlord. You want your own furniture and things about you. You want the freedom of having friends to stay without worrying about any busybody finding out.

Since then, of course, it's dawned on me that from the financial aspect, buying a house was the best thing I'd ever done. I have the option of buying out my friend if she wants to leave, which I could do by extending the mortgage. Even if we sold up, I could buy elsewhere, since the house has increased in value over the years.

We chose somewhere which gave us each a kitchen, bedroom and living room, with only the bathroom to share. That way we both have our privacy as well as the security of knowing there is another person around if you need them. It's nice if you are ill, for instance, to have someone to pop out and do a bit of shopping for you.

I also know now that I don't want children of my own. I don't think I'm prepared to make the kind of sacrifices I think you should make if you are going to be a good parent.

I've grown fairly selfish living on my own and being able to please myself. I would be very reluctant to have to give up my career, and having no family responsibilities has made it much easier to be singleminded not only about work but about getting involved with all kinds of local activities connected with the school. I enjoy these very much.

A lot of my maternal instincts are satisfied by my work. I'm certainly not bereft of children – working with them all day I get lots of hugs and kisses; I delight in all the funny little things they come out with. In fact, I get all the nice bits without having to cope with the nasty ones.

As to managing on my own, well, I don't mind handling money. I don't like it when the fence falls down and I have to find someone to come and fix it, but on the other hand, I'm glad I can. Sometimes I think it would be nice to have a man around who would simply take all that kind of thing over – but if I ever start going out with a fellow who looks as if he's going to I get resentful!

You don't have to be lonely because you are single. It's not difficult to meet fellas – just difficult to find one you'd want to settle with. Most of the ones I meet tend to be younger – I'm currently going out with one who is twenty-six. He sent me a lovely birthday card which said 'Women are like bustlines – only interesting when they are over thirty-four'.

The thing is, I'm not sufficiently motivated to go out looking for someone who would make a suitable husband, if such a thing exists. A lot of men are very wary of women with money, careers and a home of their own. But why should I want to give up any of that?

And I do like my own company. After a hard day at work there's nothing better than to come in, eat a whole tin of something out of the kitchen cupboard if I feel like it, then lie in the bath and have a good soak without worrying about what anyone else wants to do. It's bliss.

*Sandy* is thirty-two, an unmarried mother with a daughter, Janey, who is six. They live in a council flat and Sandy is a local authority social worker. She says:

I was living with someone when I got pregnant with Janey, but the relationship had already reached the rocky stage and the pregnancy turned out to be the last straw. I never really considered abortion. I wanted the baby and felt I would cope somehow.

Looking back, my attitude seems amazingly naïve. I had no experience of small children, let alone babies, and after the birth I don't really think I knew what had hit me. I was lucky in a sense, in that I had a job I could go back to after maternity leave and we were able to find somewhere to live.

But I had not realized just what an emotional and physical strain it would be looking after a newborn baby all on my own. Now, I have no regrets. We made it somehow and Janey and I are very close. Of course, I have all the single-parent hassles of child minders and school holidays. You do find yourself asking a lot of favours from friends. But, luckily, I seem to be blessed with some very good ones.

My mother was very much in favour of abortion at the time. She told me that no man would want a woman with a child. In fact, I haven't found that a problem; quite the reverse, if anything. Lots of men I know seem to relate very well to children. The danger has been that I would choose a a man simply because he seemed to get on well with Janey – that nearly happened once. I almost agreed to get married – then I realized it wasn't something you should do to find a father for your daughter, but because you wanted it for yourself.

In fact, I'm not sure I could settle into that kind of one-to-one togetherness any more. I've got too set in my ways. And I look at some of my married couple friends and ask myself what they've got that I haven't. Sometimes, it seems, the women have a much rougher time. On the surface it looks as if they've got a husband, but underneath all they've really got is another big kid.

*Maureen* is forty-three, divorced, with two grown-up children. When her marriage broke up three years ago she agreed to the sale of the family house, moved into a two-bedroomed flat and trained as a word processor operator. Now, she says, she has never been happier.

I'm not saying there haven't been some bad moments; there have. For the first year after the divorce I felt a real failure. The only thing I knew was to be married and I hadn't managed that too well, it seemed. I felt very bitter, very hurt. My husband had decided to trade me in for a new model and the only bright spot that year was when I heard that she, in turn, had left him for a younger man.

Financially, my husband was very generous. I didn't have to work, but I wanted to. Just as I didn't have to leave the house, but I couldn't bear the thought of living there alone after all those years, looking at all the things we'd chosen together.

In the event, I think moving out and getting a job were the best things I could have done. For the first time in twenty years of being married I started to think about me for a change.

I gradually got more self confidence and I even stopped worrying about what effect the divorce woul have on the children. My eldest son told me recently that he thought his father and I should have split up years ago – he said I was a much nicer person to be with now! I'd always handled the household budget and since my husband was hopeless around the house I did most of the painting and decorating, so that side of things wasn't a problem when I started to live alone.

The hardest part was making new friends. Most of the people I knew when I was married were other couples. And although they were all very kind, after a while you began to feel a little bit awkward. And most of the women at work were much younger than me. In the end, I swallowed my pride and joined a local club for the divorced and separated. Despite my fears, it wasn't full of cranks and misfits and I've made some good friends there – male and female.

Of course, I get lonely at times. But my husband was often away on business when I was married, so being lonely is nothing new. And the other side of the coin is the amazing freedom you have knowing you don't have to please anybody about anything, except yourself.

Barbara, Jill, Sandy, Maureen: four women with their own perspectives on being single. But all would agree that being successfully single, happily single, depends on your state of mind. It is seeing being alone as solitude rather than loneliness; it is enjoying one's independence rather than feeling one is struggling to cope.

There never was a better time for a woman to be single and this book aims to help you make the most of it. It is not aimed specifically at the single woman who is thinking of marriage, or the married woman in the throes of divorce, or the girl who wants to know the pros and cons of living with her boyfriend. There are other books on these subjects and there is a brief reading list at the end of this chapter. But for every single woman who, in the words of Helen Gurley Brown, has to face dragons or make a living, and who wants to reach, stretch and grow, this book is a basic survival guide.

### Books on living together

Pat Clayton, *The Cohabitation Guide*, Wildwood House.
Clare Dyer and Marcel Berlins, *Living Together*, Hamlyn Paperbacks.

**Books on marriage and divorce**
Maureen Green, *Marriage*, Fontana Paperbacks.
Gay Search, *Divorce and After*, Anglia Television Ltd.
Jacqueline Dineen, *Going Solo*, Unwin Paperbacks.

# 1
# The Single Woman at Home

Finding somewhere to call your own home sweet home can be fun – or it can be a nightmare. And whether you dream of renting a bedsit in a city, buying your own roses-round-the-door country cottage, or simply getting a roof over your head, you need loads of determination and bags of optimism.

Having time and money on your side helps, of course, but even if you have neither, it pays to know about all the options.

## Council housing

In general, your chances of getting council accommodation are very low. Different councils have different ways of working out the allocation of their housing stock and deciding who qualifies to go on to their waiting lists. Some, for instance, insist on a residential qualification, which means you must have lived in the area for a certain number of years before you are eligible for housing.

Since council housing is supposed to go to those most in need, single people tend to go to the bottom of the heap. However, if you are homeless or threatened with homelessness through no fault of your own AND you qualify as being in priority need, the council is obliged to find you somewhere to live under the Housing (Homeless Persons) Act 1977.

The council will want to know why you are homeless; whether you have just walked out of your home, or failed to pay the rent. They will want to know if there is a 'local connection' or whether you should be applying to some other council. They will also need to know whether you come under one of the following categories:

1. You are pregnant.

2. You are a single parent with a dependent child/children.

3. You are (or have living with you) a pensioner.

4. You have a dependent mentally or physically handicapped person living with you.

Even if a council accepts that you qualify under the Act it is unlikely to wave a magic wand and come up with a 'des. res.' with all 'mod cons'. Single people are often offered accommodation such as a flat in a block no longer considered suitable for families with children; the Act says nothing about the standard of housing offered to homeless people. There may be no permanent accommodation available, in which case the council may offer you a temporary place in a hostel or bed-and-breakfast hotel.

If you are homeless, but do not qualify to jump the waiting lists under the 'priority need' categories, it may still be worth your while contacting the council. Under the Act, the housing department is required to offer you 'advice and appropriate assistance' to help you find somewhere to live independently. The advice and appropriate assistance varies from area to area, but may include lists of estate agents, accommodation agencies, hostels and bed-and-breakfast hotels.

It may also be worthwhile contacting your local housing aid centre or citizens' advice bureau (see lists of organizations at the end of this chapter). A useful book has been produced by CHAR, the national campaign for Single Homeless People. Called *In On The Act* it describes how to go about applying for council housing if you are single and homeless, and is available from CHAR, 5-15 Cromer Street, London WC1H 8LS.

## Housing associations

Because there is such a gap between the demand for and the supply of council housing, the government set up the Housing Corporation to promote, supervise and fund housing associations up and down the country. There are now about 2,800 associations registered with the corporation in Great Britain, providing some half a million homes.

Housing associations either buy, convert and renovate older properties or build new homes, all of which they then offer to tenants at a fair rent which has been set by the local rent officer. Some associations aim specifically to help single people, while others concentrate on the needs of the elderly, for example. But, once again, waiting lists tend to be long.

The local Citizens' Advice Bureau or Housing Advice Centre should have a list of housing associations in your area or you can contact the appropriate regional office of the Housing Corporation (see the lists of organizations at the end of this chapter).

Most single women are forced willy nilly to turn to the private sector when it comes to finding somewhere to live. Then the questions are whether to rent or buy, whether to live alone or with others?

## Flat-sharing/renting

Some of my best friends are girls I met through answering one of those 'SW18 Prof F o/r lux flat £125 pcm' small ads in the evening paper. But flat-sharing can be a disaster. The first problem is finding somewhere: scour the postcards in the local newsagents' windows; get the early editions of the evening paper in your area if there is one, the weekly local paper, *The Times* or *Time Out* in London.

The initial stages can be time consuming. It is frustrating to make phone call after phone call to discover you are already twelfth on the list of hopefuls. It pays to call in response to advertisements as early as possible. Another tip is to start at the bottom of the column, not at the top like everyone else.

Arm yourself with a street map of the area you want to live in so that you can see *before* you make the first visit whether the flat is a three-mile hike from the nearest form of public transport, or under the flight path of the airport, or overlooking the motorway or flyover.

Once you visit the flat you will know from looking around whether the accommodation itself is what you had in mind. (I once spent two happy years in a flat in Kilburn where the bath was in the kitchen, but my room was huge and sunny.) Just bear in mind that it is a flat-share rule that the last in gets the smallest room!

Harder by far is to decide in the space of half an hour or so whether you will be able to co-exist peaceably with the other flat-sharers. A degree in psychology probably comes in handy at this point, but failing that, try to make sure everyone is in when you go to see the flat. Ask about their work, their social life, their friends. What are the house rules on boyfriends/visitors/paying for phone calls/splitting the bills? Little things can say a lot.

Are there milk bottles individually labelled in the fridge? Or is there a communal kitty for things like coffee and sugar? Is there a housework rota pinned on the kitchen door, or, conversely, an inch of grease on the kitchen stove?

If it is a mixed flat make sure the women are not expected to do more than their share of housework (although in my experience of mixed flats it was the women who got away with doing least).

If it is a shared house as opposed to a shared flat, find out who is responsible for the garden. It might be nice to have somewhere to hang your washing out in the summer, but not so nice if you are the mug who is always going to have to mow the lawn or do battle with the ground elder.

How much you have to pay will depend on where you want to live and the size of the property. In London, for instance, according to one of the flat-sharing agencies, you might expect to pay upwards of £35 a week plus bills for gas, heat, light etc. for a room in a flat in the area bordered by the Circle line of the tube. Elsewhere it would be £30 or less (figures for 1984). But you need quite a sizeable sum to start with – it is common to ask for a month's rent in advance plus the equivalent of a month's rent as a deposit.

In addition, if you find your flat through a flat-share agency rather than under your own steam, you may have to pay an initial registration fee of, say £3, plus a further sum once they have placed you. This could be a week's rent plus VAT.

Of course, flat-sharing is not for every woman. Other

alternatives include renting a bedsit and sharing a kitchen and bathroom, or renting a self-contained flat – and there are all kinds of permutations in between.

If you have the time and energy it is worth shopping around to find somewhere that suits you, simply because where you live can make such a difference to the way you feel.

Some landlords, for example, seem to work on the principle that tat is good enough for tenants. Others appear to believe that the nicer the furnishings, the better the tenants will care for them.

Unfurnished accommodation does give you the chance to impose your own personality on a place, but it is increasingly hard to find. It can also be initially expensive – the outgoing tenants will probably want cash for the fixtures and fittings, and the asking prices do not always seem to relate to the quality of the items concerned.

If you do not mind the thought of moving again after a relatively short time then renting someone's home while they go on holiday or work abroad can be a better bet. I once lived in a delightful house, furnished in just the way I would have chosen, while the owners spent three years in Australia.

**What if the landlord wants you out?**
Finding somewhere to rent that suits you is just one side of the housing story. What happens if the landlord decides you must leave?

Briefly, it all depends on the kind of agreement you had in the first place, but it is worth knowing that it is illegal to use *force* to remove someone against her will from residential accommodation if she originally occupied it with the owner's agreement.

That does not mean that the landlord cannot use the law instead. A lot of women who flat-share have little protection under the Rent Acts because they have no agreements of any kind in writing. Some landlords try to avoid the Rent Acts by granting 'non-exclusive licences' to flat-sharers. Each sharer is asked to sign a separate document which gives her the right to occupy the flat, but not exclusively. This kind of licence differs from a tenancy – but the distinction is not always straightforward and it may be worth your while getting legal advice on your particular case.

If you do have a tenancy, then, once again, it depends on the *kind* of tenancy you have.

### Restricted contracts

If you live in the same house or flat as your landlord you probably have what is called a restricted contract. This can either cover a *periodic tenancy* (where the letting is done by the week, the fortnight, or month, with no end date) or a *fixed term tenancy* (for example, for one year only).

If you have a periodic tenancy the landlord has to serve you with a notice to quit in writing, laid down as required by law, with at least four weeks' notice. If you have a fixed-term tenancy, no notice to quit is required and the tenancy comes to an end at the end of the fixed term.

If you do not leave after the notice to quit has expired or at the end of the fixed term, the landlord has to get a court order for possession from the county court. (The time this takes varies, but the hearing is unlikely to take place in less than three weeks unless the landlord can convince the court there are any particular reasons why the case should come up quickly.) But once the case *does* come up, the court has no option but to grant the landlord possession.

All the court may do in your favour is to postpone the date when the possession order comes into effect. The maximum postponement, however, is only three months.

### Regulated tenancies

Furnished or unfurnished flats or houses let by non-resident landlords may be covered by regulated tenancies. A new type of regulated tenancy was introduced by the Housing Act 1980 called *shorthold*.

This only applies to new tenancies created after 28 November 1980. Its main feature is that the tenancy must be granted for a fixed period of between one and five years, agreed at the start of the letting. At the end of that time, the landlord has a guaranteed right to repossession provided he has complied with certain conditions.

All he has to do is to give you, during the last three months of the shorthold term, three months' notice in writing of his intention to apply to the court for possession. If you do not leave by the date he says he will be applying, he will be able to apply. And providing that he has stuck to the letter of the law, the court must then grant him his order.

Shortholds apart, a regulated tenancy does offer the best security, but that is why so many landlords try to make sure their properties are let under some of the circumstances which put them outside the scope of regulated tenancies. They may say they provide 'attendance' – that part of your rent covers the cost of cleaning your rooms or providing linen. They may want you to sign a form agreeing that this is a holiday let, even when it patently is not.

But if you do find yourself lucky enough to end up with a regulated tenancy then the landlord must obtain a possession order from the courts before you can be made to leave – even if the tenancy agreement itself has come to an end. And he cannot throw you out just because he has fallen out with you or has found someone who will pay more rent.

The court itself may or may not grant the order – if the landlord can prove certain things (for instance, you have damaged the furniture, not paid the rent, sub-let without the landlord's consent) the court can grant possession if it thinks it reasonable. On top of these 'discretionary' cases there are ten more 'mandatory' cases, in which the court has no choice but to grant possession. These include the case that the landlord has let a house he wants to retire to, or let his home and now wants to live there again.

The law relating to landlords and tenants is pretty complicated, so if you run into problems it is best to seek advice about your particular case. Try the CAB, the local Law Centre, if there is one, or the Housing Advice Centre. You can see a lawyer for a fixed fee (see chapter five) or go to your local Rent Officer or Rent Tribunal Office.

The Department of the Environment publishes a series of housing booklets which you may find useful (see the list at the end of this chapter), but above all, remember that eviction without a court order is a criminal offence – as is harassment. So if a landlord tries to get you out without going through the proper channels, whether it is by bullying you, being violent, cutting off services like the gas or electricity, complain to your local authority. They have powers to prosecute.

## Buying a place of your own

Sometimes it is the thought of such hassles over rented accommodation that prompts women to consider the idea of buying a place of their own. Others feel that paying out rent simply helps to line the pockets of landlords: far better to put your money into bricks and mortar of your own.

It used to be quite hard for single women to get mortgages to help them buy a property, but now it is illegal for building societies, local authorities or other organizations which lend money for home purchase to discriminate against women simply because of their sex. However, that does not mean you can march into the nearest branch of any building society and expect to be handed just what you want. It pays to do your homework first.

Most building societies lend single women up to two and a half times their annual salary, so if you earn £6,000 a year you might get a mortgage of £15,000. Many building societies will only grant mortgages of up to 90 per cent, so that on a property worth £25,000 they would lend a maximum of £22,250. They would expect you to be able to meet the rest from savings, and they often prefer you to have been saving with them for some time.

The type of property you want to buy can also affect the mortgage you might get. Some societies do not like lending money on older properties or conversions, for instance. Another snag is that when they carry out their own survey on your dream home, the society may decide the asking price is too high. Instead of offering you a 90 per cent mortgage on the £25,000 the vendor wants, they may only offer it on the £20,000 they feel the place is worth at current market values.

One other factor to bear in mind is the extra money you will have to find to cover expenses such as solicitors' fees, surveyors' fees, the building society valuation, and possibly, stamp duty. It is a good idea to have a chat with your local building society manager before you even start looking at properties so that you can see how you stand. That way you will not be disappointed if you find the flat you want, only to discover you simply cannot afford it.

Building societies are not the only organizations who lend people money to buy their own homes. Banks are now providing about a quarter of new mortgage advances. Local authorities also grant mortgages and you may be able to get a mortgage through an insurance company. It pays to shop around, especially as the rate at which you will pay interest on the loan may vary from organization to organization.

There are two main types of mortgage.

*Capital repayment mortgages:* If you have one of these, your monthly payments are made up of the interest on the loan and the repayment of the loan itself (the capital). In the early years, most of the monthly payment is interest and only a tiny amount is paid off the capital, but by the end of the loan period your payment is almost all capital with only a tiny amount of interest.

*Endowment mortgages:* With this kind of mortgage you do not repay the capital gradually year by year, but all at once at the end of the mortgage term. To make sure you will be able to do this you take out an endowment policy with a life assurance company. Each month you pay interest on the loan and your insurance premium and at the end of the term (or on your death, if earlier) the Life Assurance Company pays you a lump sum.

To make the situation slightly more complicated, there are three different kinds of endowment life policy which can be used to repay a mortgage:

*A guaranteed or 'non-profit' endowment:* at the end of the term you are simply paid the amount of money you borrowed.

*A 'with profits' endowment:* at the end of the term you not only have enough to repay what you borrowed, you also get extra cash, called profits or dividends. The snag is that the monthly payments are higher.

*A 'low cost' or 'build-up' endowment:*    here, you take out a 'with profits' policy for less than the amount you borrowed. The idea is that your bonuses will build up to cover your loan and give you a bit extra for yourself at the end of the term. The premiums are generally a little less than those for a 'guaranteed' or 'non-profit' policy.

Once you have established in principle that you can afford to buy a place of your own and that you will be able to get the kind of mortgage you need, all you have to do is find it. And, as any househunter will tell you, this is not always as easy as it sounds.

Half the battle is finding a good local estate agent who listens to what you tell him about your requirements and then does his best to match you up with clients who come to him to sell their homes. It sounds simple – but lots of agents seem to rely on sending out endless lists of properties ranging from one bedroomed flats to detached mansions and leaving it up to you to decide which, if any, are worth a look.

Learn to read between the lines in the descriptions that accompany the basic details:

'Convenient position close to railway station' (main Inter City line at bottom of garden)

'Very quiet location' (miles from shops and transport)

'Close to shopping centre' (shoppers park their cars outside all day)

'Original features' (totally unmodernized)

'Much improved and extended' (previous owner was a DIY freak)

'Purpose-built flat in popular development' (constantly changing resident population)

'Needs some redecoration' (filthy)

Do not rely on a single visit before you decide that one particular property is the place for you. The character of a street can change dramatically from morning to evening. It may seem like a quiet side-road – unless you visit it during the rush hour. Then you realize local drivers use it as a shortcut, to avoid the main-road traffic jam.

And what about the pub on the corner – will the noise of late-night revellers going home from the weekly Country and Western evening bother you?

If possible, talk to the neighbours. Find out what they like and dislike about the locality. Ask how long they have lived there. It also helps to find out as much as you can about their lifestyles, especially if, as is probable, part of your property would be adjoining theirs. If your bedroom wall is someone else's living-room wall you do not really want to be forced to listen to the Rolling Stones or the Thompson Twins at 2 a.m. Or, come to that, if your living-room wall is someone else's bedroom wall you do not want them coming round, ranting and raving because *you* are playing music in the early hours.

Having done your preliminary sleuthing and made an offer which has been accepted (usually subject to survey) you need to go back to the building society or other organization concerned to fill in a mortgage application. At the same time you should contact a solicitor about the conveyancing. You can cut costs by doing some of the legal work yourself, but this can be very time consuming. Even if you rely totally on a solicitor it is probably worth getting a copy of the *Which? Guide to Buying a House*, as this takes you clearly through each stage.

Whether you have your own survey carried out on the house or flat is up to you – the building society will have its own valuation done in any case. You may know a friend who is a surveyor who will come and look at the property for you, or you may be able to pay extra for the building society surveyor to carry out a survey for you at the same time as he carries out the valuation. That can work out cheaper than having a separate survey done. You may even be able to see the survey the present owners had carried out when they bought the property, which could be helpful if they themselves have not lived there very long.

## Alternative lifestyles

Not everyone's idea of heaven is a two-up, two-down on a twenty-five year mortgage, or even a rented bedsit in a shared house. Communes and squats were not just a sixties phenomenon.

They are still flourishing today.

## Communes

There are lots of different communes and communities up and down the country, but all of them involve some aspect of communal living. Some believe in self-sufficiency and members work together to achieve this. Some believe in income sharing, or work sharing, and some share childcare. Most are critical of 'urban industrial societies' and aim to make use of our natural resources. Many communes are vegetarian, many grow their own organic food.

At Redfield, for instance, a community near Winslow in Buckinghamshire, twenty-four adults and twelve children share a fifty-roomed Victorian house, with some cottages and a stable block. There are 17 acres of land, including two woods, a 7-acre field, a ¾-acre vegetable garden and orchard and other gardens for herbs and flowers.

All ground-floor rooms in the house are for communal use – there is a laundry room, for example, and a large sitting room. Upstairs, members have their own 'units' – the size and number of rooms per unit depending on the needs of the individual, with a couple with children getting more space than a single woman.

Meals are cooked in the communal kitchen and eaten in the communal dining room. Sunday mornings are set aside for a clean-up of the house and everyone is expected to put in ten hours a month as their share of house maintenance.

Some of the members make a living at Redfield – gardening, keeping cows and sheep, writing, teaching T'Ai Chi and music. Others work full or part time locally. Others travel further afield to their jobs.

Redfield was originally bought by the Redley Housing Co-operative, half on a bank loan and half on contributions from members in the form of loans – 'loan stock'. The Co-op owns the place and members are tenants who do not own their own unit. Each new member is asked to contribute about £4,000 to £5,000 to the loan stock. These contributions are linked to the House Price Index and are repayable when anyone leaves. Besides this initial contribution, members pay rent on their 'unit'. This is calculated according to the number of adults and children occupying it and the amount of floor space.

Redfield is not simply a way of living in a large country house and enjoying the pleasures of rural life. People who live there do so because they are committed to the idea of an alternative lifestyle. But it is just one type of community that exists. A list of places that are looking for members is published from time to time. Called *Communes Network*, it is available from Some People In Leicester, 89 Evington Road, Leicester.

## Squats

Squatting is not for the fainthearted. To join or set up a squat you have either to be desperate or very committed. Committed, that is, to the principle that it is better to use houses that would otherwise remain empty while people stay homeless.

Essential reading for would-be squatters is the *Squatters Handbook*, available from the Advisory Service For Squatters, 2 St Pauls Road, London N1 (Telephone: 01-359 8814). This gives tips on how to:

—find an empty house
—find out who owns it and what its future is likely to be
—get inside and secure the premises
—deal with the police
—get gas and electricity connected
—fight eviction

As the book points out, since the great Squatting Movement reached its peak in the 1970s, the law has been changed and the only properties worth squatting now are those owned by councils or housing associations which are likely to remain empty or undeveloped for some considerable time. These are usually in such poor condition that the owners cannot claim tenants are waiting to move in and thus have no grounds on which to have squatters evicted. But this also means that a good deal of work may have to be done before the place is really fit to live in.

This is one reason why squatting is usually a group activity – to do up a dilapidated house you need more than one pair of hands. You also need the safety of numbers to make sure that someone is in the property at all times – absentee landlords can enter by force (or get their agents to do so) and put all your belongings out on the street if no one is there.

In some of the inner cities, including London, *short-life housing* groups have grown up, partly as one way of controlling squatting. Councils and some housing associations agree to let property which is empty (but intended for redevelopment or refurbishment) on a short-life licence to a responsible group. Rents are very low or non-existent, but all repairs and maintenance are usually carried out by the people who move into the property and not the council or other landlord.

## Furnishing and decorating

Even if you are not planning to join a squat or take on short-life housing, knowing a bit about DIY can be useful. If you cannot face taking up an evening class, perhaps you can rope in a friend to give you some tips. Better still, buy a basic book or get one from the library – there are plenty to choose from and then you will not look a fool as you learn how to tell the difference between a nail and a screw.

With all the modern power-tools on the market it is unnecessary to use brute strength to sand floors or put up shelves, but if you do not want to spend your hard-earned cash on gadgets you will get little use from, consider the possibility of hiring tools as and when you may need them. Find your nearest hire shop by looking under Hire Services in the Yellow Pages.

Employing workmen, whether it is to install central heating or fit cupboards in your kitchen can be a hit and miss affair. Ask friends and neighbours if they can recommend anyone and, where possible, find a firm that belongs to a trade association such as the Federation of Master Builders or the Institute of Plumbing. It is no guarantee that things will not go wrong – but it may give you a better chance of redress if they do.

Always get several written estimates before you employ anyone to take on a large job and remember that cheapest is not necessarily going to be best.

It is worth building up a good network of craftsmen such as electricians and plumbers, if only because firms who specialize in 24-hour emergency services can work out very expensive. In any case, it is a good idea to find out – before disaster strikes – where and how to turn off main supplies like gas, water and electricity, and how to do basic things like changing a plug, mending a fuse and unblocking the sink. Your electricity board showroom has leaflets explaining how to deal with plugs and fuses, and as for the sink, a lot of boiling water and a big plunger bought from your local hardware shop will often do the trick.

Decorating your home is a question not just of your budget, but of your imagination. Of course, if you are in rented accommodation the landlord probably has strict rules about what you may and may not do, but it is always worth asking if you may paper or paint a room. Provided your taste is not too extreme he or she may be only too willing for you to improve the state of the place at no cost to them.

Another possibility is to camouflage as much as you can. Hide the hideous kitchen lino under rush matting. Cover the sofa with lace shawls and cushions. Even plain stretch loose covers can improve the looks of a garishly patterned three-piece suite.

Furnishing a home need not break the bank either. Scan the 'Articles For Sale' columns of your local paper. Jumble sales and junk shops can also be treasure troves and if there is a local auction house near you could pick up lots of bargains. Most auction houses have a day when you can view and, at the same time, leave bids with the auctioneer so that you do not actually have to go along in person. There is usually a list which will give you an idea of the price an item is expected to fetch, so that you can adjust your offer accordingly.

Another source of bargains can be secondhand office equipment suppliers. I once bought six pretty bentwood chairs from one of these places – a snip at £12, particularly since they turned out to be originals, made by Thonet, the man who invented the bentwood process, and worth far more than I had paid for them!

## Where to go for help

CHAR:    the campaign for single homeless people, 5-15 Cromer Street, London WC1H 8LS, 01-833 2071.

SHAC:    the London Housing Aid Centre, 189a Old Brompton Road, London SW5 0AR, 01-373 7276.

Housing Advice Switchboard:    (telephone advice only) 01-434 2522.

SHELTER:    the national campaign for the homeless has housing aid centres in Birmingham, Bristol, Manchester, Newbury, Sandwell, Taunton, Plymouth, Welwyn Garden, Swansea and the Rhondda Valley. Local details from Shelter, 157 Waterloo Road, London SE1 8FX, 01-633 9377.

Check your local phone directory for your local housing aid centre or contact the local CAB. The National Association of Citizens' Advice Bureaux can give you their number and address.

NACAB is at Myddelton House, 115-123 Pentonville Road, London N1 9LZ, 01-833 2187.

The Housing Corporation, 149 Tottenham Court Road, London W1P 0BN, 01-387 9466, has regional offices in Croydon, Exeter, Leicester, Wolverhampton, Leeds, Liverpool, Manchester, Edinburgh, Glasgow and Cardiff.

Law Centres Federation, Duchess House, 18-19 Warren Street, London W1P 5DB, 01-387 8570, will tell you your local law centre if you cannot find one listed in your local phone book.

Advisory Service for Squatters, 2 St Paul's Road, London N1, 01-359 8814.

## Useful reading material

Publications by SHAC include:
  *Buying a Home*
  *Rights Guide for Home Owners*
  *Somewhere to Live in London?*
  *Private Tenants: Protection from Eviction*

Booklets published by the DOE and available from them or local
Rent Officers include:
  *The Rent Acts and You – a brief guide for landlords and tenants*
  *Letting Rooms in Your Home*
  *Shorthold Tenancies*
  *Notice To Quit*

The Consumers' Association publishes:
  *The Legal Side of Buying a House*
  *Raising Money to Buy Your Home*
  *Which? Way to Buy, Sell and Move House*
  *The Which? Book of Do It Yourself*

# 2
# The Single Woman at Work

Gone are the days when work was just a stopgap between leaving school and getting married. These days work plays an important part in a single woman's life.

It is not just the would-be career women, who see themselves as high powered, high earning, high flyers, who need to think carefully about the kind of job they want. More and more women carry on working after they are married and have children. More and more women find they need to go back to work after divorce.

So, whether you are a single girl looking forward to the independence that first pay cheque will mean, or a woman who suddenly finds herself single and needs to get back into the labour market, think hard before you take the first job that comes along, even in times of high unemployment. For, despite Women's Lib, despite the sex discrimination laws, and despite the equal pay acts, women tend to end up in low-status jobs – with low pay. Often we only have ourselves to blame. We just do not set our sights high enough, and we often underplay the skills we have.

Can you drive? What about becoming a sales representative, a chauffeur, a lorry driver? Good at organizing? How about taking a a mangement training course? Be a boss, not a secretary.

Think about the future – computers and electronics are growth industries and will need skilled technicians. At the same time there will always be a need for craftspeople – could you be a carpenter or a furniture restorer?

If you still have no clue what to do, do not panic. There are lots of places to go for help and advice.

*Careers Offices:* There are around 1,000 in the UK and although they are mainly there to help school and college leavers, they may be able to help you if you are going back to work after a gap. If they cannot help they will give you advice on who can. Find them by looking under the name of your local education officer in the phone book.

*Jobcentres/Employment Offices:*   These government-run centres can be found in every town and city. Apart from displaying jobs, the centres can also advise on training courses which may give you the skill to get a job you would like. The Training Opportunities Scheme (TOPS), for instance, offers full-time courses lasting from between a month and a year and can be great for women who want to train in 'men's' jobs such as car maintenance, engineering or joinery.

*Professional and Executive Recruitment (PER):*   If you have some qualifications and/or experience they will help you find work in the professional, managerial, executive, scientific and technical fields. They put you on their mailing list so that you get a copy of *Executive Post*, a weekly, nationwide paper with up-to-date job vacancies listed in it and advice on how to apply. PER also organize seminars offering advice on job hunting, letter writing, form filling, interview techniques and so on. Check the phone book for your nearest office.

*Private Recruitment Agencies:*   These can be found in most parts of the country, but the service they offer can vary enormously. Some agencies take great trouble to try to match your skills and requirements with job vacancies available. Some seem to delight in sending you off on one wild goose chase after another. Agencies are licensed by the Department of Employment and cannot legally charge you, the job seeker, a fee for finding you work.

When you are looking for for a job, do not forget that under the Sex Discrimination Act it is illegal for any employer to treat a woman less favourably than a man would be in the same situation. There are some loopholes, of course, including jobs where the 'essential nature' of the work calls for a man for reasons of 'physiology'. This would apply to modelling, for instance, or acting – but not to jobs where sheer brute strength or stamina were important. In those cases each applicant would be judged on his/her own merits.

Other exceptions to the Act include:

—jobs in private households,
—jobs where other men would fear for their decency or privacy,
—jobs in firms where fewer than six people are employed.

The Sex Discrimination Act does more than lay down the law about the recruitment and hiring of staff; it also applies to the way you are treated once you have been given the job. Under the Act you must be given the same chance as men for training, and you must be equally considered for promotion or transfer. You cannot be made redundant simply because you are a woman, nor can you be sacked on the grounds of your sex.

More information about the Act can be obtained from the Equal Opportunities Commission (see the list of addresses at the end of this chapter) and this is also the body to contact if you feel you have been discriminated against. They can give you free advice and, in many cases, financial assistance if you have a case to take to an industrial tribunal.

If you feel you have been discriminated against you have to make a complaint to an industrial tribunal within three months of the incident. You may feel you want to try other channels first – your employer's grievance procedure, if there is one, or getting your trade union, if you are a member, to intervene.

To start legal proceedings you need to obtain an IT1 form from the EOC, any Jobcentre or unemployment benefit office and send it to the Central Office of Industrial Tribunals, whose address is given on the form. At the same time – or even before – you can get a questionnaire (called 'Sex Discrimination Act 1975 – the questions procedure') which will help you find out why you were treated the way you were and may help you to decide whether to go ahead with your claims.

Get two copies of the questionnaire and complete them both. Send one to your employer (it is probably a good idea to send it by recorded delivery) and keep the other for reference. The EOC can advise you about the questions you should ask. Employers do not have to reply – but failure to do so could be used against them in evidence at any later tribunal hearing.

Once you have completed form IT1 and sent it off you set the legal ball rolling. A copy of your complaint goes automatically to the Arbitration, Conciliation and Advisory Service who will then get in touch with you to see if a settlement can be reached without the need for a tribunal hearing.

It is up to you to decide whether to settle or to go ahead. No one can force you to agree to anything at this stage if you do not want to. But you should already be clear in your own mind as to what you hope to achieve.

You can claim three separate things:

1. An order declaring your RIGHTS.

2. An order for COMPENSATION.

3. A recommendation for a course of ACTION.

Compensation could cover lost earnings, damages for injury to your feelings, or damages for future loss of earnings. The 'course of action' could include being offered the next suitable vacancy (if you were turned down for a job) or being considered for promotion within the next year (if you had been passed over previously).

## A contract of employment

When you start a new job you may not be given a written contract of employment straightaway. But if you turn up for work having been told what your duties are, what hours you will do and how much you will be paid, that verbal agreement still constitutes a contract.

However, in most cases, you should get a *written* contract within the next thirteen weeks. This statement has to give certain information about your job and it also has to include a note on disciplinary and grievance procedures – or tell you where to go to check these out.

It must give your job title; how much and when you are paid;

hours of work; holidays; what happens if you are sick; what kind of pension scheme operates; and notice periods required. It must also give you the date when your employment began and say whether any job with a previous employer counts as part of your 'continuous period of employment'.

Presumably, if the terms and conditions had not been right, you would not have taken the job in the first place. But it does pay to check your contract carefully. Your job title may seem a little vague, for example. Could your employer later change your duties?

You may also find that the hours or rates of pay are not as good as those applying to men doing the same job. In that case you might be able to make a claim under the Equal Pay Act.

## The Equal Pay Act

Although there is an Equal Pay Act most women would agree that we still do not have equal pay. Women's average weekly earnings are still only 66 per cent of men's, according to the Trades Union Congress. One of the reasons is that the jobs traditionally done by women are the low-paid jobs, the dogsbody jobs like cleaning, clerking, catering.

Even where men and women do the same kind of work, men are more likely to be in the better paid grades. The TUC discussion book *Working Women* points out that:

—Male nurses earn £3.15 an hour on average, female nurses £2.70 an hour,
—Male shop assistants earn £2.50 an hour on average, female shop assistants earn £1.70 an hour.

New regulations amending the Equal Pay Act came into effect in January 1984 and many campaigners for women's rights were hoping that these would help women use the law more effectively for a fair deal. (In 1981, only six of the equal pay cases heard by industrial tribunals were successful.)

The new regulations allow a woman doing a different job from that of a man to claim that her work is equal in value to his. If you want to make a claim under the Equal Pay Act to an industrial tribunal, get advice from the EOC or ACAS (see the list of addresses at the end of this chapter).

Another reason why women do not do as well as men when it comes to pay is that they do not chase promotion or do as much overtime. Many of them work part-time or on a casual basis as 'temp' secretaries, for example, or agency nurses.

Often it is not that women lack the ambition or drive. But they may be holding down another job – that of mum. And for the single working mother, in particular, life can be tough.

## Maternity leave and pay

You cannot be sacked because you are expecting a baby – or, at least, if you are, you can generally claim unfair dismissal. And you are also entitled to reasonable time off work, with pay, to have ante-natal care.

Under certain circumstances, however, your boss could ask you to leave and the law would give you no protection. For instance, to be covered by the law you must have worked for the same employer for at least a year, or, if he employs fewer than twenty people, at least two years. If you work between eight and sixteen hours a week the qualifying time is five years.

Your boss may also be able to claim that your pregnancy makes you incapable of doing your job properly or that it is actually against the law for you to carry on in your present job while pregnant. Under those circumstances he has to try to find you alternative work to do while you are pregnant – on similar terms and conditions as your present job – and your rights to maternity pay and returning to your original job after having the baby are not affected. A typical case might be that of a radiographer, who, by law, cannot be exposed to radiation during pregnancy, and so could not work normally again until after the baby is born.

If you do think you have been unfairly dismissed because of your pregnancy you can complain to an industrial tribunal. Even if your boss can prove dismissal was fair for one of the two reasons given above, you can still complain it was unfair if you know there was a suitable alternative job available, but you were not offered it. In any case, you must complain within three months of the dismissal.

If the tribunal decides in your favour it can order your boss to reinstate you or take you on in a similar job, if that is what you want. If this is impractical or if you do not want to go back after all, it can make a cash award in compensation.

If you are having a baby, when you stop work and when you start again may depend on all kinds of things. But you are only legally entitled to a maximum of eleven weeks before the birth and twenty-nine weeks afterwards. (Of course, you can take less than this if you want.) If you are ill, whether or not this is connected with your pregnancy, you can extend your leave by four weeks. Unless your union or your company has its own maternity agreement, only six weeks of this leave will be paid.

It does not matter whether or not you intend going back to work – you still qualify for maternity pay if you have worked for the same employer for two years from the eleventh week before the baby is due (if you work sixteen hours or more a week) or if you have worked for the same employer for five years from the eleventh week etc. (if you work between eight and sixteen hours a week).

The same conditions apply in order to qualify for maternity leave and the right to return to work, but to make sure you keep this right you have to tell your employer THREE times that you intend to do so.

The first notification must be in writing and must be given three weeks before you intend to stop work. In the letter you must say that you are stopping work because you are going to have a baby, that you intend to return to work after a period of maternity leave, and you should also include the expected date of confinement.

After you have had the baby you may get a letter from your employer asking you to confirm that you intend coming back to your job.

You must write back within fourteen days or you could lose your right to return. Finally, at least twenty-one days before you intend to start work again you must write to let your employer know the date on which you propose to return.

Useful booklets on the subject include *Employment Rights and the Expectant Mother*, published by the Department of Employment, and *Parenthood in the Balance* published by the EOC (see lists of addresses at the end of this chapter). Both set out the law and a woman's rights quite clearly, although the EOC booklet is more readable.

One of the points the EOC make is that Britain still lags behind most of Europe in its provisions for women who want time off to have babies. For the single woman who becomes a single mother, getting back to work may be a financial necessity, but it can also be a nightmare. And the once-married, but suddenly single, woman who also needs to work again can face the same kind of problems: what to do about the children.

## Childcare

In general, employers do little to help the single working mother – there are a handful of crèches and nurseries run by enlightened employers but these are for the lucky few.

Costs vary considerably, but an average charge to the mother would be around £10-12 a week plus extra for meals. Sometimes employers subsidize the cost of a certain number of places in local authority or privately run nurseries, but now that the taxman has decided that this is a 'perk', and therefore a taxable 'benefit in hand' like a company car, single mothers may no longer find this the godsend it once was.

In any case, there are just not enough places to go round. Relatively few nurseries – whether state or privately run – will take children under two; nor are your problems over once children start school. The school day is much shorter than the average working day and then there are the school holidays to consider.

Contact the Social Services department for details of nurseries in your area. Help and advice can also be sought from Gingerbread, a self-help organization for single-parent families, and from the National Council for One-Parent Families (see list of addresses at the end of this chapter).

If you cannot find a nursery, or if no place is available, you could consider a *childminder*. The local Social Services department should have a list of registered childminders and they may be able to tell you which ones have vacancies and whether they can take a child the age of yours.

A *registered* childminder is one who has been vetted by the Social Services and whose house has been checked for space, cleanliness and safety. She may have had no formal training, but she may well have been on a special course. She has probably had children of her own and may have been a nursery nurse or a teacher.

The idea is that you take your child to her house before you go to work and collect him or her when you get back at night. Usually childminders are registered to look after no more than three children under five, including their own under-fives, but they may also look after older children before and after school and during school holidays.

If you are considering getting a childminder to look after your child, then it is worth having a look at a leaflet produced by the National Childminding Association, called *I Need a Childminder*. This guide answers most of the questions you will have.

Sometimes it may be more convenient for you to have your child cared for in your own home. That is when you turn to the ranks of au pairs, mother's helps and nannies. There are pros and cons to all three – it is up to you to weigh up the odds. Au pairs suffer from homesickness, get entangled with unsuitable boyfriends and leave you in the lurch sometimes – but then, so do 'nice' girls from Lancashire. And if you have older children, an au pair who gets time off to study during the day but is there when the kids come home from school may be what you need.

If you have a small baby it might be reassuring to know that he or she is in the capable hands of a trained nursery nurse or nanny. But you will have to pay for that training – it is not only Norland nannies who expect £60 plus a week wages. Do not forget, too, that experience can be worth as much, if not more, than formal training. A girl who has looked after lots of young children may be better than a girl who has just come straight from college with her qualifications still hot off the presses.

You can find your 'treasure' by going through agencies (if you can afford their fees) or by the time-honoured way of advertising in *The Lady*. If you get a copy from your local newsagent you will be able to work out current hours and conditions from the columns of existing ads.

According to the nannies and mother's helps I have talked to over the years, that I and my friends have employed, it pays to be specific in your own advertisement. As one girl said:

> I always look at the semi-display advertisements first (the ones in little boxes). People have allowed enough space to tell you a little bit about themselves and if they are prepared to spend a little bit more then they cannot be mean. When you think about it, they are looking for someone to take care of their children. It should be important to them; not worth scrimping on.

Of course, the cost of having live-in help like nannies or mother's helps makes it impossible for many single women to consider the possibility unless they are themselves fairly high earners. It is not simply a question of wages: you have to live somewhere big enough to give the girl a room of her own, you will have to face extra heating and lighting bills if girl plus baby are at home all day, and you will be feeding an extra adult.

For the woman who is single *and* a mother there are no easy ways to carry on working, particularly full-time. And part-time work is generally hard to find, poorly paid, carrying few fringe benefits and without much job security.

Also the kind of jobs offered to part-timers tend to be the less skilled – cleaning, catering, shop work. If you have secretarial skills then 'temping' for an agency may suit you, but there is no guarantee of regular work; at the end of the day the pay always seems to be less than you expected and, of course, you rarely get sick pay or holiday entitlement.

A better way of working part-time is to 'job share'. Job sharing is an idea which is very successful in America but is still in its infancy in Britain. Basically, two part-time workers share one full-time job between them. Not only does each have the advantage of working a shorter number of hours per week, but both get security of tenure, holiday pay, sick pay and so on.

Job sharing has been arranged at the Stock Exchange, the House of Commons library, social work departments, law centres, doctors' surgeries and in service jobs. But very few private companies have introduced the idea, and if that is where you work then you have to persuade your bosses that the idea can succeed. First of all you will have to find your 'other half'. Then you will have to work out the hours each would work, how you would liaise, what sort of responsibility each would take and so on.

The Equal Opportunities Commission publishes a booklet on job sharing and you can contact a charity called New Ways to Work (347a Upper Street, London N1; telephone: 01-226 4026) for help and advice. For people living in the Greater London area they also run a register to match would-be job sharers. This costs £2 to join or 50p for the unemployed.

Getting a job, knowing your rights, and getting back to work as a single mum – these are just three aspects of knowing how to survive at work. But what happens if you weather all these hazards only to find yourself beleaguered by the unwanted attentions of the men you work with – your boss, your workmates or your subordinates?

### Sexual harassment

Sexual harassment is one of those topics that often produces sniggers rather than sympathy. But for women who have to endure it such harassment can make working life a misery and it can be difficult to know how to handle. Nor do you have to be a Dolly Parton look-alike to be on the receiving end.

Unfortunately, a lot of people feel that women who complain about sexual harassment are making a lot of fuss about nothing. They may be accused of not having a sense of humour or of wanting to take the fun out of life. But there is a big difference between harassment and flirting or banter, where a woman can give as good as she gets and can enjoy the light relief this provides.

Sexual harassment is persistent, unwanted sexual advances or sexually explicit derogatory statements – and it is more widespread than many people realize. A Marplan poll revealed that one in ten women workers felt that a man had been taking advantage of his position at work to make persistent advances. Another survey, carried out by the Alfred Marks Bureau, one of the bigger employment agency chains, found that 51 per cent of women had experienced some form of sexual harassment in their working lives. This ranged from being eyed up and down (only 4 per cent saw this as harassment), to being touched or patted (42 per cent), to being made a direct sexual proposition (82 per cent).

The survey said:

> According to both employees and management, sexual harassment has an adverse effect on the work of one in five victims; one female office manager lost interest in work because she realized it would be impossible to get promotion without sleeping with the boss. Other women admitted to a lack of concentration or a refusal to work overtime for fear of being alone in the office with a few men.

Psychologists say there are three main motives for sexual harassment: the simplest is sexual desire – lust looking for satisfaction. The second is personal power. A boss may harass a woman working for him to make himself feel more important, more virile, more in control of his domain. The third motive is social control. Harassment is a safe weapon for a man who thinks women should not be out at work. Since he can no longer legally discriminate against women, he can use his position or authority to embarrass or humiliate them and perhaps even get them to leave. Even if this does not happen he has 'put them in their place'.

To any woman who is being sexually harassed, the reasons WHY do not usually matter: what is important is HOW to handle the situation. A victim will generally do one of four things: put up with it in the hope that the offender will eventually stop; approach the offender direct; complain to a superior; or, often as a last resort, change jobs.

The National Council for Civil Liberties has come up with some tips on how to go about whatever course you decide. These are contained in a leaflet called *Sexual Harassment at Work*. They include:

—Checking with other women to see if they have had to cope with similar behaviour from the same man. Work together if possible – that way you gain support and self confidence.

—Asking the harasser to stop behaving in ways that offend and upset you. Be specific – many men do not realize that jokes and touching in particular circumstances are offensive. If you can, get a friend or collegue to be there when you speak to the man.

—Collecting evidence of harrassment. Write down what is said or done and when. Ask a friend or colleague to take a note as well. Then, if necessary, approach the relevant boss or manager to see if the situation can be sorted out.

—If you belong to a union, asking officials to raise the matter at section or branch level. Get your union to work out a policy on sexual harassment if one does not exist.

—Contacting the National Council for Civil Liberties or the Equal Opportunities Commission for advice and suggesting to management that it is in their interest to have a procedure that deals with sexual harassment.

One possible solution, if all else fails, is to take legal action. But relatively few cases involving sexual harassment have been heard in Britain and these have all been taken under the section of the law relating to unfair dismissal.

The women involved either claimed they were forced to leave their job because of sexual harassment or that refusal to comply with sexual demands was the reason for their dismissal.

For instance, a nineteen-year-old girl went to work as a clerk in a small builders' merchants. She claimed that her boss never left her alone. He slapped her bottom, brushed against her and kept touching her. Finally she told him to stop, but his response was to tell her she should think herself glad to work in such a happy environment. She then stormed out in a temper telling him to 'stick his job'. Later, an industrial tribunal ruled that her boss's advances amounted to unfair dismissal – and he was ordered to pay her £954 compensation.

## Useful addresses

Equal Opportunities Commission: Overseas House, Quay Street, Manchester M3 3HN, 061-833 9244.

National Advisory Centre on Careers for Women: Drayton House, 30 Gordon Street, London WC1H 0AX, 01-380 0117.

Professional and Executive Recruitment: Rex House, 4-12 Regent Street, London SW1Y 4PP, 01-930 3484.

Advisory, Conciliation and Arbitration Service (ACAS): head office at 11-12 St James Square, London SW1Y 4LA, 01-214 6000.

National Council for Civil Liberties: 21 Tabard Street, London SE1, 01-403 3888.

Gingerbread: 35 Wellington Street, London WC2, 01-240 0953.

National Council for One-Parent Families: 255 Kentish Town Road, London NW5 2LX, 01-267 1361.

## Useful publications

*Fresh Start*, an EOC booklet for women who want a new, better paid, more worthwhile job, dealing with training schemes, further education and grants.

*Train For a Better Job with TOPS*, available from local Jobcentres.

*How to Prepare Your Own Case for an Industrial Tribunal*, an EOC guide to procedures.

Employment Legislation Booklets from the Department of Employment, Caxton House, Tothill Street, London SW1, 01-213 3000.

*I Need a Childminder*, National Childminding Association, 204 High Street, Bromley, Kent BR1 1PP, 01-464 6164.

*Sexual Harassment at Work*, a TUC Guide for trade unionists, from the TUC, Congress House, Great Russell Street, London WC1B 3LS.

# 3
# The Single Woman and Sex

The Sexual Revolution of the sixties probably put paid once and for all to the notion that 'nice girls don't' – at least, not before they have an engagement ring on their finger. According to the survey carried out by *Woman* magazine in February 1984 very few single girls today plan to save sex for marriage. But the survey also showed that in other ways attitudes have not changed all that much.

It may be all right for a man to sow wild oats; but women who play the same game are still dubbed 'promiscuous'. The old double standards persist. So, although in theory today's single woman is free to choose the sexual lifestyle that suits her, in practice this is not always the case.

Whether she wants the freedom to have lots of different sexual partners, or whether she wants to say 'no' to sex altogether, the single woman can find herself under all kinds of pressures to change her mind. Instead of liberating single women, the sexual revolution may have trapped them. For years newspapers, magazines and sex manuals have been preaching the message that sex is fun, just another skill to be learned like driving a car or cooking a meal.

The emphasis has been on technique – how to have better, more frequent orgasms, how to make love in fifty-four different ways. Sex has been seen as a purely physical experience and one which women – freed from fear of pregnancy by the Pill – could enjoy just as much as men.

But many women found that things just did not work out that way. Far from enjoying this new sexual freedom, it actually made them miserable. While they might not want to turn the clock back, they often found themselves under pressure to have casual sex when, perhaps, they did not want to. Where once a man would worry about contraception, now he assumed a girl was on the Pill. Where once he would have thought himself lucky to get a goodnight kiss on the first date, now he expected breakfast in bed the next morning.

The fact is that men and women do not always see sex in the same way. Many women do not enjoy one-night stands or casual encounters – the sex that is best for them is the kind that takes place within a loving relationship.

## First experiences

The *Woman* survey underlined this. It revealed that the most common time for a single girl to have her first sexual experience is between the ages of sixteen and eighteen. Of these girls, around three in five did so because they were in love or because of the way they felt about a particular boyfriend, even if they did not call it love. One in five wanted to see what sex was like and the rest said they were talked into it or had been drinking.

But the significant fact is that over half of the women who made love because of the way they felt about their boyfriend found the experience enjoyable. Less than a quarter of those who were 'just curious' did so and the vast majority (89 per cent) of those who were talked into sex did not enjoy it at all.

Most women who have not had sex look forward to the 'first time' as something special. In fact, it is often quite a disappointment. The survey also showed that the younger you are when you first make love, the less likely you are to enjoy it. Of course, this may have something to do with the fact that young lovers rarely have their own double bed in which to take their time: sex can be rushed, surreptitious. But the younger you are, the less likely you are to know your own sexuality, to be aware of the way your body responds or to be confident enough to tell your partner what is nice for you.

Legally you are not supposed to have sexual intercourse until you are sixteen. In practice, lots of girls do. Estimates vary – one survey by *Loving* magazine put the figure at 48 per cent of teenage girls. Other national surveys put it as low as 6 to 12 per cent.

If you do have under-age sex you could be taken to court by your parents, the police or the social services department if your local council thinks that you are in 'moral danger'. The court might pass a supervision order, appointing a social worker to keep an eye on you for a certain period, or it may pass a care order, placing you in the care of the local council. The council then decides where you live – at home, in a hostel or a 'community home'.

The boy or man you have been sleeping with may be prosecuted, although in practice if you are having sex with someone of your own age, rather than an older man who might be seen to be 'seducing' you, this is probably unlikely.

Another good reason for not rushing into sex at an early age is that you may be putting yourself at risk of various physical problems. For instance, women who become sexually active when they are young, and who have a number of different sexual partners (inevitably, the two are often linked) run an increased risk of cervical cancer. The more sexual partners you have, the more likely you are to catch one of the sexually transmitted diseases; there is a greater risk of pelvic infection which can affect your chances of having children later.

Saying 'no' to sex is not always easy. Men still come out with the same old lines: 'What's wrong with you, are you frigid?', 'You would if you really loved me'. It is hard to hide behind the old excuse that you are frightened of having a baby, since his response is bound to be 'Well, why don't you go on the Pill?'

There are no perfect ways of dealing with the situation. So much depends on the individual relationship. But the main thing is to try to make it clear you are not rejecting the man, simply the sexual experience.

Be as honest as you can. If you like going out with a man, but simply do not fancy him you should make it clear that what you want is friendship rather than passion. (You may lose a friend, but that's probably better than a wrestling match at the end of each date.) If you simply feel the relationship is too new, or that you are not ready, then say so. Make it clear you are not saying 'never' but, for the time being, 'not yet'. (But do not use this as a ploy for keeping some poor guy on a string – there is a name for women like that.)

And it may be corny, but it is still true; if a man really cares about you as a person as well as a sexual partner, then he *will not* try to force you into anything against your better judgment and he *will* want lovemaking to be something you BOTH want and enjoy.

## Developing a good relationship

To get the best out of a sexual relationship it pays to understand your own sexual chemistry. The first thing is to know how your body works. Sheila Kitzinger's book, *Women's Experience of Sex*, has a good chapter on this.

You can get a hand mirror and examine your genitals. Learn where your clitoris is, how it responds to different kinds of touch. For most women, stimulation of the clitoris is the key to orgasm. And there is no need to feel guilty about giving yourself pleasure.

All the studies ever carried out into female sexuality show that masturbation is normal and that the majority of women have done it at some time. Most doctors and sex therapists agree that it is good for you. Dr David Delvin says: 'There are a number of benefits. It reduces tension, puts you on the right route for having an orgasm during intercourse and it helps young women get accustomed to their own vaginas.'

It also helps to become aware of the way your sexual rhythms can fluctuate from day to day, week to week. Some women feel sexiest during their periods, others around the time of ovulation. If you suffer from pre-menstrual tension then you may feel you cannot bear to be touched during this time. (Taking vitamin $B_6$ tablets can sometimes help.)

It is also worth exploring how your emotions affect your sexuality. If you feel tired, worried, even angry, you are not likely to feel like sex. The feelings you have for your partner can affect your love life and it is as well to realize this.

Of course, not all women find themselves attracted to men. It is easier than it used to be for women to have open, sexual relationships with other women, but it can still be difficult to admit to yourself, let alone your friends, your family or your workmates that you are 'different'.

There are no laws against lesbianism between women over sixteen, but prejudice still exists. Many women find it helps to get in touch with others by contacting a lesbian group or phoning a lesbian befriending service. There are some telephone numbers at the end of this chapter.

Knowing your own sexual needs is one thing – getting the kind of sex you want within a relationship is another. Many women find it hard to talk about sex with their partners. They feel shy or embarrassed or they are afraid that they will upset the other person by making them feel a failure.

Counsellors who work with couples experiencing sexual problems suggest a number of ways to go about changing things if you are not happy with your sex life:

1. *The carrot not the stick*
The idea is to reinforce the behaviour that pleases you and ignore that which does not. So you react positively to things that turn you on – you say 'That's lovely' or murmur with pleasure. And you bite back comments like 'Don't do that'.

2. *Choose your moment*
Do not wait until your partner is actually panting with passion before you mention the fact that his technique could do with a little improvement. Try to find a time when you are feeling close and comfortable – but not actually leading up to love. And talk about the way YOU feel, not the things HE does. That way you will not put him on the defensive right away.

3. *Be assertive – not aggressive*
Telling a man he is a rotten lover and has never given you a moment's real sexual pleasure is hardly going to improve the situation. He will just feel hostile or humiliated rather than loving and willing to please you. Work out how you would like things to

change and take one step at a time.

Start with something easy – far better to begin by telling your man you *like* something he does (kissing your neck, for example) and would like him to do it more often, than to make your first move by asking him *not* to do something.

### 4. *Teach him about touch*

Men often fail to understand the importance to a woman of what is called 'foreplay'. In fact, many women find this as satisfying as intercourse itself. Even men who do realize that few women like the wham, bam, thank-you ma'am, approach, often believe that twiddling a woman's nipples or clitoris for a few minutes will do the trick and turn her on.

But you can show men that the whole body can become an erogenous zone. One way of doing this is to give him a massage and then get him to give you one too. Or start lovemaking in the bathroom, gently soaping each other's bodies.

## Where to turn for help

There are lots of ways you can try to sort out your sex life yourself and there are lots of books which can give you ideas on how to do it (see the list at the end of this chapter). But if you decide you want to seek professional advice, being single is no problem.

So where can you go?

*Consult your own GP:* Your doctor can make sure there are no physical reasons why you are not enjoying sex properly. She can also refer you to a psychosexual specialist or a clinic attached to a local hospital. Of course, you may feel the last person you can talk to about your love life is the family doctor. You may even feel guilty about taking up her time when you are not really 'ill'. In that case, you could approach a clinic direct.

*Local clinics:* There is now a wide choice of clinics up and down Britain, so you should be able to find one within striking distance. But waiting times vary – it could be a matter of weeks before you get an appointment, or it could be up to six months. Some clinics are run by the NHS, others are private. Some are attached to family planning clinics, others are youth advisory clinics for young people.

To find those near you, contact your Area Health Authority or the Family Planning Information Service in London.

*Family Planning Clinics:* Even if your local FPC does not specialize in sexual problems by running special sessions, there may be one doctor who counsels perhaps one afternoon a week. This is worth checking out.

Although you do not have to be married to get help, it is better if you go along as a couple. A spokeswoman explained:

> We do feel that a sex problem is usually a couple's problem.
>
> We get a lot of single women ringing us up but it's terribly difficult to help them until they find a steady partner. If a woman does have a regular boyfriend it's best if he can be persuaded to come to therapy sessions too. If he says it's not his problem – that the woman's frigid, for instance – we suggest she asks him along under the pretence of giving her moral support.

*Marriage Guidance Council clinics:* Despite the name, the MGC will help single people with sexual problems, although they also find it most helpful to deal with couples. Apart from general counselling, available at any MGC, there are a number of sexual dysfunctions clinics around the country. You can find your nearest by ringing your local MGC or the national head office.

*Youth advisory centres:* In some areas these are run by the local authority. Elsewhere there are private ones like the Brook Advisory Centres, set up specifically to help young people with emotional and sexual problems (see the list of addresses at the end of this chapter).

At Brook, counsellors are quite happy to see single girls alone. As a spokeswoman explained:

> We make no demands. We are aware that young, unmarried girls are probably happier coming to us anyway.
>
> Quite often a problem can be cleared up in a half-hour

chat. A girl may come in for the Pill and admit she's not really enjoying sex and never has. You may find she's got a vague hostility towards her boyfriend – perhaps she feels he doesn't show her enough affection. But he may think it's 'soft' to cuddle her. So we advise her how to get him to show his feelings, instead of just jumping into bed with her.

The techniques we use vary according to whatever is appropriate. If more than just talk is needed then more than just talk is offered. For instance, if a girl has vaginismus (involuntary clenching of the vagina that makes sex painful or even impossible), or if she's uptight about her body, we may teach her to touch herself. We get her to use a speculum so that she can see what her cervix looks like.

The kind of sex therapy on offer throughout the country tends to be either 'speech therapy' or the use of techniques pioneered by the US sex researchers, Masters and Johnson, now generally referred to as 'sensate focus'.

Speech therapy is simply another way of saying that people are encouraged to talk through their problems, to understand them and to deal with them themselves.

As a spokeswoman for the NMGC said:

Much of our work deals with helping couples to communicate. Often they don't know how to use the words. We get them to discuss the feelings they have, their fantasies, what they'd like their partners to do to them. If you can get a couple talking like that, often the difficulties will melt away.

We also use Masters and Johnson techniques. We might start by banning sexual intercourse altogether, and making them go back to the beginning of a relationship before they were making love.

The idea is to have lots of cuddles and kisses, to rediscover the pleasures of each other's body without having to go as far as making love. Only after some days, or even weeks of these 'sexercises' is the couple given permission to have full sexual intercourse. The idea is that by working up to this in stages, the stress is removed, and a couple can relax and learn to enjoy sex.

Few single women will be able to relax and enjoy sex if they are worrying about getting pregnant. And 'taking a chance' is simply not worth it. Of the 2,000 single women who sought abortion advice from the Pregnancy Advisory Service over the course of one year, failure to use contraception was the overwhelming cause of pregnancy.

There are still a lot of myths about when you can and when you cannot get pregnant. So it is worth knowing that you *can* get pregnant:

—even if you do not have an orgasm,

—even if you are standing up (standing on your head or in any position),

—even if it is your first time,

—even if you were having a period,

—even if he never fully penetrated you,

—even if he was 'careful',

—even if you douched afterwards.

You can get contraceptive advice and supplies free: it does not matter whether you are married or single, in a steady relationship or not. You can either go to a GP or to a family planning or young people's clinic.

Most GPs give birth control advice and supplies. If yours does not, or if you do not want to see your own GP, you can go to another doctor for this service. You can sort out which GPs offer family planning services by checking the lists of GPs kept in libraries or post offices or by contacting your family practitioner committee. Those who give contraceptive advice are identified by the letter 'C' after their name.

Alternatively, there are about 2,000 free family planning clinics in the UK. You can get addresses and times from health centres, hospitals, libraries, Yellow Pages or the phone book by looking under 'family planning' or by contacting the Family Planning Information Service.

There are pros and cons in choosing either a GP or a clinic. Your GP probably knows more about you than a clinic doctor, although you will be given an examination at a clinic and asked for details of your medical history. If you go to your GP you will probably see him every visit: at a clinic you may see different doctors and nurses.

On the other hand, your GP will not prescribe sheaths and may not be able to fit you with an IUD. He may have to refer you elsewhere. Also, you will have to take your prescription to a chemist; at a clinic you can usually walk out with the contraceptives you need. In addition, if your GP has been your family doctor, you might feel uncomfortable going to him for contraceptive advice.

If you are under sixteen and want contraceptives or contraceptive advice, things have become much more complicated since 1984. Prior to that, any doctor who prescribed contraceptives to a girl under sixteen had no legal obligation to get her parents' consent before doing so. The DHSS guidelines said the whole question was an ethical, rather than a legal one.

However, in December 1984, the Court of Appeal ruled that a doctor must not prescribe contraceptives or give contraceptive advice to a girl under sixteen, without her parents' consent, except in an emergency or with the leave of the court. At the time of going to press, the Government was planning to appeal to the House of Lords to get this judgement overturned but in the meantime the official guidelines on contraceptive advice for young people had been suspended. Doctors could still prescribe contraceptives to girls under sixteen, but if they did not get the consent of their parents they ran the risk of being sued for damages by parents in the civil courts.

It is quite possible that the situation will now have returned to the way it was before, but, in any event, there are several points worth making. Young girls often worry about the confidentiality aspect – but this should never really have been an issue. The British Medical Association has said that consultations between a doctor and a patient should always be confidential, no matter what age the patient is. If you are under sixteen and ask a doctor about contraceptives he should not tell your parents about your request, even if he says he cannot advise or prescribe without their consent. However, it is worth knowing that some clinics are probably not going to insist on seeing your birth certificate or a written form of parental consent.

Obviously, it is best if your GP knows you have been prescribed the Pill or fitted with an IUD by a clinic (in case any other treatments or conditions are affected). And, in most cases, the clinic doctor will write to your GP. But if you do not *want* your GP to be told, then you can make this clear.

## Methods of contraception

Choosing the best kind of contraception for you is something that depends on a variety of factors. The doctor will help you decide. The main thing is to be as happy as possible with whatever method you choose – if you do not feel comfortable with a cap, for instance, you probably will not use it properly and you will risk pregnancy.

### The Pill

The most popular type of contraceptive in Britain is the Pill. The combined Pill, which contains two hormones, oestrogen and progestogen, is almost 100 per cent effective. It works by stopping ovulation. The mini-Pill, which contains progestogen only, is 98 per cent effective and works by causing changes in the body which make it difficult for sperm to enter the womb or for the womb to accept a fertilized egg.

The main advantage of the combined Pill, particularly for single women, is its effectiveness, combined with the fact that it is easy and convenient to use. It does not interfere with the spontaneity of lovemaking and it means that your monthly cycle is always regular, always predictable. However, like all drugs, the Pill can produce side-effects which may range from nausea and weight gain to thrombosis and high blood-pressure. This is why it is important that before taking the Pill you discuss your personal and family medical history with the doctor.

In general, the combined Pill is thought less suitable for women over thirty-five, particularly if they are overweight or if they smoke. The mini-Pill may be prescribed instead, as it carries less risk of high blood-pressure and blood clotting problems.

Some recent studies have suggested that there is a link between cancer and the Pill. An American study – based on a small sample of 314 breast cancer patients – suggested that women who had been taking Pills with a high progestogen content for more than five years, before the age of twenty-five, were four times as likely to have breast cancer as women in the control group. And an English study suggested there might be a link between long and early use of the Pill and cervical cancer. The Family Planning Information Service says:

> Whether or not the Pill is a contributing factor to breast cancer, there is never any good reason for taking a high dose drug where a low dose is effective. Talk it over with your doctor.
>
> As for cervical cancer, the problem is that many of the factors which are linked with early and prolonged use of the Pill (early sexual activity, for example, and several sexual partners) have also been found to be linked with cervical cancer.
>
> In any case, whether or not the Pill is a contributing factor to cervical cancer, the disease is preventable and if women have regular cervical smears they can detect the possibility of cervical cancer *before* it occurs.

If, after weighing up the risks and the advantages, you decide the Pill is not for you, what are the alternatives?

### The Intra-uterine Device (IUD, IUCD, the Coil)
*Effectiveness:*    96-98 per cent
*How it works:*    The plastic or plastic and copper device is inserted into the womb by a doctor. Some women feel minor discomfort as this is done, others quite severe pain. No one is sure exactly how it works, but it may stop a fertilized egg implanting in the womb.

*Advantages:*    Once the device is in place, you do not have to worry about it – so it does not interfere with lovemaking. You do not have to remember to take it every day like the Pill, or put it in every time like the Cap.

*Disadvantages:* It increases your chances of getting a pelvic infection – which may leave you sterile. So unless you never want children or have completed your family choose another method. Doctors used to fit single women with IUDs without worrying too much; now many refuse to do so. Other risks include perforation, expulsion of the device and getting pregnant while it is still in place. If this happens, the chances of an ectopic pregnancy are higher than usual. (In an ectopic pregnancy the baby grows in the Fallopian tube.)

## Barrier methods (the cap or sheaths plus spermicide)

*Effectiveness:*   97 per cent with careful use.

*How they work:*   Sperm warfare: The idea is to prevent the sperm from getting into the womb. The spermicide attacks and the cap or sheath defends. Other barrier methods now include throw-away spermicide-impregnated sponges. These are eighty-five per cent effective on average although some studies show a failure rate as high as twenty-seven per cent.

*Advantages:*   Apart from the slight possibility that you might be allergic to some spermicides or the rubber used in the cap or sheath, there is no risk of side-effects. In addition, there may be some protection against cervical cancer and/or sexually transmitted diseases.

*Disadvantages:*   May interrupt lovemaking, can be messy, and/or embarrassing to use unless you are very at ease with your body and that of your partner. Many men object to using sheaths as they complain it reduces the sensation. Caps must be checked regularly to make sure they still fit. Sheaths can tear or burst.

## The safe period

*Effectiveness:*   Some find it 85-93 per cent safe with careful use.

*How it works:*   The aim is to predict ovulation and to avoid intercourse when a woman is most fertile. This is done by charting your body temperature before you get up each morning and by noting changes in your vaginal mucus.

*Advantages:*   No mechanical devices or hormones are involved.

*Disadvantages:*   Unless you have a regular and ordered life, and regular cycles, it is very difficult to do properly. Even within a steady relationship it can be stressful knowing there are days when lovemaking is forbidden. In addition, illness, stress etc. can affect your cycle, making it even harder to be sure it is safe to make love.

### Sterilization
*Effectiveness:*   Very occasionally the tubes rejoin and fertility returns.

*How it works:* The Fallopian tubes are cut or burned so that the egg cannot travel down them to meet the sperm. Once this has been done the chances of having the operation reversed are relatively small, so it must be seen as a permanent method.

*Advantages:*   Once done, you do not have to worry about contraception again.

*Disadvantages:*   You cannot change your mind about wanting children. Single women may find it hard to persuade doctors that they seriously do not want children, or have completed their family.

From this brief summary of the types of contraceptive available it is clear that there is no one perfect answer. What may suit a single girl in her twenties – the Pill, for example – may not be so advisable in later years.

Many women find that during their lives they switch from one method to another as their lives and circumstances change. Yet, however carefully women try to plan their lives, accidents *do* happen. Women forget to take the Pill, or they get hit by a sickness bug and realize belatedly that they should have taken extra precautions the night before. They meet someone at a party, fall in love and into bed without stopping to think of the consequences. Sheaths burst, caps can perish and spermicide run out at the most inconvenient times.

If this happens to you then you can take emergency measures. The *morning-after Pill* can actually be taken up to seventy-two hours after unprotected intercourse, but, obviously, the sooner you take it, the more effective it is likely to be. The treatment is actually two tablets of a fairly high dose combined Pill, followed by two more after twelve hours. Side-effects include nausea and, occasionally, vomiting.

The *morning-after coil* is an ordinary IUD inserted a day or two after unprotected intercourse. Of course, once it is there you are stuck with it until you go back to have it out – you cannot really view it as a short-term measure.

You should be able to get the morning-after Pill from your GP or your local family planning clinic. Whether you think the Pill or the coil would be best, the important factor is time. If you cannot get an urgent appointment to see a doctor, or if your doctor or clinic do not fit IUDs, phone one of the private or charitable organizations which offer a post-coital service to find out whether there is a clinic near you. (Addresses and the phone numbers for the Brook Centres, BPAS, PAS and Marie Stopes are at the end of this chapter.)

Whether you use the Pill or the IUD for post-coital contraception you will probably be asked to go back a month later to make absolutely sure you are not pregnant. It is also a good idea to make absolutely sure by then that you are using a reliable form of contraception – so that you do not face any more emergency measures.

## Sexually transmitted diseases

While today's freer attitudes mean that a single girl can find sex fun, she can also find it more risky, too – in the sense of contracting a sexually transmitted disease (STD).

Herpes is the new scare word – but the other diseases are still around: syphilis, gonorrhoea, NSU, trichomoniasis. And it is no good telling yourself that 'nice' girls do not get diseases. Anyone with more than one sexual partner, or with a sexual partner who is not wholly faithful to them, is at risk. According to most experts, the number of patients attending STD clinics is now the highest ever – but this may simply reflect a more responsible attitude to what used to be called venereal diseases (VD) rather than an epidemic. Certainly, if you are at all worried that you might have contracted some kind of disease it is worth going straight to one of these clinics. Your GP will probably refer you there anyway and their facilities for testing are far greater than the ones your GP has to hand.

A wide variety of infections fall within the province of the STD clinic and it may be that you are suffering from some type of vaginal infection which is not sexually transmitted at all. You will not be made to feel a nuisance even if it turns out you are in the clear, so if you do start to suffer any symptom that is unusual or suspicious, have it checked out. To find your nearest 'Special Clinic' or STD clinic, phone your local hospital or contact the Family Planning Information Service. Treatment is free.

*Thrush* (also known as monilia or candida):   This is actually a tiny fungus and the commonest infection for women to catch. It causes a variety of symptoms from pain, to itchiness, and a thick, white discharge. Doctors usually prescribe nystatin in the form of pessaries or cream, or you may be given tablets to take by mouth. Alternatively, you might like to try putting natural yogurt in your vagina every day instead, and if you are prone to repeated attacks it is best to wear cotton panties and stockings rather than tights.

*Trichomonas* (also known as TV):   This can cause a very painful and irritating discharge, which may smell nasty and look yellow or greenish and bubbly. Treatment is a course of Flagyl tablets, which usually docs the trick.
*NB:*   even if your partner has no symptoms he should have a course of tablets, too, as he could keep on re-infecting you.

*Syphilis:*   This is now a fairly rare disease in Britain. Between one and a half and thirteen weeks after having sex with an infected person you develop a hard painless sore, which later becomes a kind of raw spot. In women this may be hidden deep inside the vagina and may go unnoticed. If this is untreated, a few weeks later the secondary symptoms appear – maybe a slight rash, mouth ulcers, spots or sores. A course of high-dose penicillin injections nearly always cures syphilis.

*Gonorrhoea* (also known as the clap): This is still a very common infection. You can catch it, not simply from ordinary sex, but from oral or anal sex. Men who catch it usually notice a thick yellow discharge and pain when they urinate, but in women the early symptoms are far less definite. There may be pain when urinating and a vaginal discharge but anything up to 50 per cent of infected women have no idea anything is wrong until the disease is quite far advanced. By this time the infection may have spread to the Fallopian tubes and ovaries, causing lower abdominal pain, fever, irregular periods and vaginal discharge. There is also a risk of infertility. Penicillin and other antibodies are usually used although more resistant strains of bacteria require stronger drugs.

*Herpes:* This is a virus infection which can either affect your face as a cold sore or your genitals as genital herpes. Both types can be passed on by direct physical contact and infection shows up as little clusters of red patches with blister-like sores. The blisters go away in roughly two weeks, but the virus simply lies low in the body and re-emerges from time to time. So far, there is no cure for genital herpes – you simply have to learn to recognize the warning signs that herald an attack (maybe itching, tingling, tenderness) and avoid sex until you are clear again so that you do not infect others. There is a drug called acyclovir which can reduce the severity of the attack and scientists are working on vaccines.

*Non-specific urethritis (NSU):* This is mostly a male disease and the symptoms are similar to those of gonorrhoea. It seems as if the micro-organism chlamydia may be responsible for many cases of NSU – and possibly for many cases of tubal infection and sterility which occur in women. Many women show no symptoms and although the infection is easy to treat with tetracyclines it is not always easy to diagnose. As always, if your partner is found to have some kind of infection or STD, then you should go for a check-up too.

*Lice and scabies:* Pubic lice cling to the pubic hairs and are passed by sexual intercourse or sharing a bed with someone who already has them. They are usually too small to be seen and the only symptom is itching. Various creams or lotions can be prescribed to get rid of them. Scabies is caused by mites which burrow under the skin to lay eggs. They also make you itch like mad – not just in the genital area but anywhere they make for, often the wrists, fingers, elbows, armpits. They, too, can be caught by simply sharing a bed with an infected person and treatment is much the same as for lice except that the lotion has to be spread all over the body.

## Useful addresses and phone numbers

Family Planning Information Service: 27 Mortimer Street, London W1N 7RJ, 01-636 7866.

Regional Family Planning Association centres' telephone numbers:

| | |
|---|---|
| Bedford | 0234 62436 |
| Brighton | 0273 774075 |
| Glasgow | 041-333 9696 |
| Norwich | 0603 28704 |
| Belfast | 0232 225488 |
| Birmingham | 021-454 8236 |
| Exeter | 0392 56711 |
| Cardiff | 0222 42766/7 |
| Liverpool | 051-709 1938 |
| Sheffield | 0742 21191 |

National Marriage Guidance Council: Herbert Gray College, Little Church Street, Rugby, Warwicks CV21 3AP, 0788 73241.

The Scottish Marriage Guidance Council: 26 Frederick Street, Edinburgh EH2 2JR, 031-225 5006.

Clinics offering birth control advice and post-coital contraception include:

Marie Stopes House: 108 Whitfield Street, London W1P 6BE, 01-388 0662

Brook Advisory Centres:

Central Office: 153a East Street, London SE17 2SD, 01-708 1234.

Birmingham: 9 York Road, Birmingham B16 9HX, 021-455 0491

City Centre Brook, Top floor, 8-10 Albert Street, Birmingham B4 7UD, 021-643 5341.

Handsworth Brook Centre, 102 Hamstead Road, Handsworth, Birmingham B19 1DG, 021-554 7553.

Saltley Brook Centre, 3 Washwood Heath Road, Saltley, Birmingham B8 1SH, 021-328 4544.

Bristol: Brook Advisory Centre (Avon), 21 Richmond Hill, Clifton, Bristol BS8 1BA, 0272 736657.

Coventry: Gynaecological Outpatients, Coventry and Warwickshire Hospital, Stoney Stanton Road, Coventry, 0203 412627.

Edinburgh: 50 Gilmore Place, Edinburgh EH3 9NY, 031-229 3596.

Merseyside: Brook Look-In, 9 Gambier Terrace, Liverpool L1 7BG, 051-709 4558.

London: 233 Tottenham Court Road, London W1P 9AE, 01-323 1522 for inquiries, 01-580 2991 for appointments.

Also, telephone Tottenham Ct Rd for appointments at:

—Shoreditch Brook Centre, 210 Kingsland Road, London E2 8EB.

—Barnsbury Centre, Barnsbury Clinic, Carnegie Street, London N1 9QW.

—Newham Centre, 84 West Ham Lane, Stratford, London E15 4PT.

Islington Brook Centre, 6-9 Manor Gardens, London N7 6LA. 01-272 5599

Brixton Brook Centre, 53 Acre Lane, London SW2 5TN. 01-274 4995

Walworth Brook Centre, 153a East Street, Walworth, London SE17 2SD, 01-703 9660 or 703 7880.

Telephone Walworth Brook Centre for appointments at:

—Stockwell Brook Centre, Rose McAndrew, Community Health Service Clinic, Beale House, Lingham Street, London SW9.

—Lewisham Brook Centre, Lewisham Hospital ante-natal department, Lewisham High Street, London SE13 6LH.

—Kennington Brook Centre, Moffat Health Centre, 65 Sancroft Street, London SE11 5NG.

—Wandsworth Centre, St Christopher's Health Centre, Wheeler Court, Plough Road, London SW11 2AY.

British Pregnancy Advisory Service: Austy Manor, Wootton Wawen, Solihull, West Midlands B95 6BX, tel: Henley in Arden 3225.

For a full list of branches, see the list of addresses at the end of chapter eight.

Lesbian Lines (women only switchboards) – days and times vary:

| | |
|---|---|
| London: | 01-251 6911 |
| Bradford: | 0274 42895 |
| Liverpool: | 051-708 9552 |
| Manchester: | 061-236 5986 |
| Newcastle: | 0632 618555 |
| Birmingham: | 021-622 6589 |
| Cambridge: | 0223 246113 |
| Glasgow: | 041-221 8372 |

A full list can be obtained from Gay Switchboard, 01-837 7324, or from *Gay News* or *Gay Times*.

## Useful books/publications

Dr David Delvin, *How to Improve Your Sex Life*, NEL.
Celia Haddon, *The Limits of Sex*, Corgi.
Sheila Kitzinger, *Woman's Experience of Sex*, Dorling Kindersley.
Penny Kane, *The Which? Guide to Birth Control*, Consumers'
  Association.

Pamphlets available from the Family Planning Information
Service include:
  'Morning-After Birth Control'
  'There are 8 Methods of Birth Control'
  'The pill'
  'Intrauterine devices'
  'Barrier methods of birth control'
  'Family planning using the "safe period"'
  'Introduction to Family Planning'

# 4
# The Single Woman and Men

Today's single girl does not automatically feel she needs a man as a kind of accessory to make her life complete. The very young may still score status points among their peers according to the kind of looks or job their boyfriend has, but most single girls are very well aware of their own independence and individuality, and hesitate to describe themselves as so-and-so's girlfriend, fiancée or mistress.

However, the smart single girl, while not desperately trying to avoid spinsterhood or a lonely old age, is well aware that there is nothing so exhilarating as a love affair, that life can be even more fun if there is someone to share it with. Every woman knows how deliciously wicked it can be doing things when you are entirely on your own – eating baked beans cold out of a tin, watching 'Dallas' without interruptions, reading a trashy novel in the bath. But equally, there are times when solitude can seem more like loneliness.

That is not to say that finding a man is the answer to every problem. In fact, for the suddenly single – the newly separated or divorced – the prospect of any permanent relationship may well be something to shy away from in the immediate future. But the power of sexual attraction being what it is, few women would want to spend the rest of their lives without male contact of any kind, whether it is sharing a pint at the local with the lads or an idyllic fortnight for two on a holiday isle in the sun.

So, sooner or later, whether you are after Mr Right or not, you have to face up to the question: how does a single woman meet men?

Organizing a social life when you are young may not be too much of a problem. It is all very well for people to suggest that single women can go to discos, singles bars, wine bars and all the other traditional man-catching haunts, but, unless you have a friend or group of friends to go with, the prospect can be daunting to say the least. You are more likely to have a girl friend in the same boat if you are in your teens or early twenties, but if you are single and older your friends tend to be married or part of an established couple. This means that they are either constantly fixing you up with a series of nice men to meet (usually mutually embarrassing) or else they see you as some kind of threat, a man-eater with an eye for their own men.

But whatever your age and circumstances, it is no use sitting at home over your cocoa moaning that you never meet any nice men. After all, if Cinderella had not gone to the ball, she would never have met her Prince. And while you may not have a fairy godmother to help, there are other ways of magically giving yourself the confidence to get past your front door.

Someone once said that most women would starve to death if they looked for jobs the way they look for men. And there is a lot of truth in this. The trouble is, when it comes to the opposite sex, a self-sufficient, organized woman can turn into a shy, dithering, irrational heap of nerves.

The first thing is to realize that meeting a mate is really a matter of mathematics. Despite all the fairy stories, there is no one ideal man made just for you. Given the right circumstances, there are many men who could be your match. And the more men you meet, the more likely you are to find one of them. So do not be discouraged at first if you simply seem to attract all the others. There is a T-shirt slogan that sums it up: 'To find your prince you have to kiss a lot of toads'.

Once you have grasped that basic idea, you then have to turn your attention to yourself and your own attitudes to the relationships between men and women. From early childhood most little girls are conditioned to see their own success or failure in terms of male approval. Never mind that a five-year-old girl is a whiz at tree-climbing or playing with the home computer, the chances are that she will not be Daddy's rascal or Daddy's little genius – she will be Daddy's beauty or Daddy's darling. At an early age she learns that male approval often has more to do with how she looks than what she does.

As she grows up, the message is hammered home by the teenage comics which suggest (simply by ignoring all other aspects of female life) that the only important things revolve around the boy-meets-girl scenarios. Advertisements tell us that we only have to wear the right swimsuit, drink the right diet colas, or use the right make-up, to have men flocking round us. The implication is that it is how we look that counts, not what we are.

The liberated lady may recognize this for the nonsense that it is. But it may help to know that research has shown men do not actually go for women who are especially sexy or particularly beautiful. Stunners make most men nervous. What attracts them is a girl who responds to them – and if she is bright and self-confident they will be even more flattered, and interested.

So try and do away, once and for all, with the idea that your worth can be measured by the kind of man you have in tow. And if there is no man in your life at present, that simply means that you have not met one yet whom you would like to be with – nothing more, nothing less.

Do things to boost your ego that do not depend on getting male approval – work for promotion or go for a better job. Become an expert at something – aerobics, silversmithing, whatever. Take control over your own life. And put the whole question of meeting and attracting men in perspective. After all, you do not expect to go through life getting on with all the women that you meet. Why should you expect your relationships with men to be any different? Sometimes you will 'click' and sometimes you will not.

Once you have enough self-confidence to get out there and start meeting men, how do you go about breaking the ice? There is nothing worse than walking into a party, glass in one hand, handbag in the other, only to be confronted by groups of people who all seem to know each other. Or sitting opposite a fascinating man in a train but being too crippled with shyness even to smile at him.

The first thing to tell yourself is that most men like being chatted up. A survey carried out by the *Sun* newspaper showed that 81 per cent of single men approved of women who made the first moves – and 72 per cent would like to go out with such a girl.

The second thing is to ask yourself what would be the worst thing that could happen if you actually walked over to man, smiled and introduced yourself? Or spoke to a stranger on the train about the weather? You could be snubbed, or ignored. Or perhaps fobbed off after a few minutes' polite conversation. But would that really be so disastrous in the grand scheme of things? Studies have shown that people who have the most satisfactory relationships with the opposite sex are not the most witty, or the most successful or the most beautiful, but the ones who are the most persistent, the ones who know that for a certain number of 'no's you will eventually get a 'yes'. They have learned to accept a 'no' without feeling personally rejected and without turning one minor disappointment into a major tragedy.

You can learn to do this too. After all, there could be all kinds of reasons why a man fails to respond to your show of interest in him, apart from the conclusion to which you immediately jump (i.e. 'he finds me uninteresting or undesirable').

—maybe he is married and faithful,
—maybe he is about to be made redundant and worried sick,
—maybe he is coming down with flu and feels rotten,
—maybe his mother just died,
—maybe he is terribly shy.

The point is, you will never know why – and so there is no point agonizing about it. And there is certainly no point going home in a deep depression believing that just because one man did not fancy you, you must be a total failure as a woman.

Another thing to remember, if you find it hard to strike up casual conversations, is that most people – and that includes most men – like to talk about themselves. So learn to be a good listener. Have a stock set of questions you can pop in at the right time. Does he live nearby? Has he always lived in this area? What is his job? Does he enjoy it? Does he drive? What sort of car has he got? What kind of music does he like? He looks pretty fit – how does he keep in shape? If he answers in monosyllables, cut your losses and move on. But if he shows he is interested do not spoil things by making him feel trapped. There is no reason why you cannot follow up the first meeting a few days later – by asking him for a date.

These days there is absolutely no reason why a single girl should not ask a man out. But there is a right way and a wrong way. So when you summon up the nerve to pick up the phone and dial his number:

—Do not chat on vaguely for ages without coming to the point,
—Do not ask 'What are you doing on Saturday night?' That is simply putting him on the spot,
—*Do* suggest something specific on a specific date.

If you do not have the nerve simply to ask him to the pictures you can always say you have been given tickets for a show and wondered if he would like to come. Or if you feel that is still too direct, arrange to see the film with a group of friends and then ask him if he would like to join you all.

Of course, you could ring him up and ask him round for a meal but that can be tricky. He might run a mile from any scene that smacks of cosy domesticity or he might equally assume that you will be on offer along with the after-dinner-mints. One way of avoiding either possibility is to issue a daytime rather than an evening invitation and to make it a friendly gathering rather than a romantic tête-à-tête. Ask him to Sunday brunch. Tell him you are having a few friends over and you would love it if he could come and meet them. Or explain that you are organizing a Saturday lunchtime barbecue – would he like to come and bring some sausages?

By arranging things this way you are keeping things casual – and you stay in control. Neither of you has to decide straightaway how involved you are going to get – sexually or otherwise – but you do get a chance to know each other.

Of course, there are some types of men who are better avoided altogether, however attractive. They simply spell trouble.

*The Married Man:*   Even if you do not know beforehand that this one has a wife and two children tucked away somewhere, he is fairly easy to spot. If you meet him in a pub after work he always knows the times of the trains back to Purley, Hemel Hempstead or some similar family-style suburb where he lives. If he takes you out for a meal it is to some obscure restaurant where the lighting is so low that it is hard to read the menu let alone see who is eating at the next table. His shirts tend to be nicely ironed and he always has a clean handkerchief. His socks come in pairs, too; you will never catch him wearing one navy and one dark grey. There are other giveaways to be spotted if he gives you a lift in his car – babywipes in the glove compartment, sweet papers on the floor, straps on the back seat that could restrain a carrycot.

To some single women a married man might seem to offer fun without strings. But beware. It is very easy to get hooked.

And whatever he says, most married men do not, repeat NOT, leave their wives. You may get an extra thrill at first from the atmosphere of secrecy that surrounds your affair until you realize that you will never be able to introduce him to your family or friends and you will be unlikely to meet his. You will probably spend hours waiting for the phone to ring and when it does he may well be cancelling your next date because the children have measles or he has to go to a school concert.

The chances of your spending a whole night together are minimal and weekends are entirely out. When you are in love with a married man Sunday afternoons can be the loneliest time in the world. You will be alone, too, at Christmas, Easter and all the other family holidays and although you will be expected to be understanding about his commitments, heaven help you if he finds out you have accepted an invitation out with another man.

*The Newly Divorced Man:* He is the kind of guy you might meet in the launderette, trying to figure out how much washing powder to use. Or the type who launches into a bitter attack on the whole legal profession when anyone mentions lawyers. He probably knows the location of every MacDonalds in the area and the opening times of the local museums and afternoon showings at the cinemas (that is where he takes his children on the afternoons he has access.)

He will either treat you very badly, because he is bitter about women in general, or else he will use you as a shoulder to cry on, going over and over the events that led to the break-up of the marriage and the terms of the divorce. If you are not careful you will end up cooking his meals, washing his shirts and soothing his soul. And for what? You will never just be a couple. If he stays with you, you will not only be gaining a lover but his ex-wife, step-children, and so on. And unless he has had time to sort himself out – at least six months on his own – you will also be inheriting all the mixed-up feelings he will still have about his marriage. It is hardly a recipe for a successful relationship.

*The Mother's Boy:*   There is a saying 'if a man's good to his mother, he'll be good to his wife'. But that is taking a long-term view. As far as girl friends go, you will have to be content to take second place.

Mother's boys do not take you out for lazy Sunday picnics, they drag you off to their mum's for Sunday roast and then spend the rest of the afternoon cutting her lawn.

Mother's boys do not make good mates for independent working girls because they have never learned to wash their own clothes, cook their own meals or clean the bathroom. They have never had to. And if you suggest it is high time they learned, you will end up on the wrong side of the woman who really counts. And unless *she* likes you, you might as well throw in the towel.

If you go away on holiday with a mother's boy he will spend half his time worrying whether she is all right back home – that is if he does not suggest bringing her along too. And you can forget any ideas of spending Christmas ski-ing in Switzerland or Easter lazing on a Greek beach: Mum always does the works on high days and holidays and woe betide you if you suggest it would not really matter if he missed out on Mum's chestnut stuffing or Simnel cake for just one year.

*The Hobbyist:*   Like all the other types of men to be wary of, this kind will have you playing second fiddle. Not to another woman, however, but to a hobby.

If the hobby involves some kind of sport, the risks may not be too great. Even the most dedicated amateur usually only spends one night training, and one or two afternoons a week playing. It is best to check this out before you become involved. It is also worth being wary about feigning an enthusiasm for the sport just to catch the man. Watching cricket on a sunny Sunday afternoon may be one way to get a tan, but how many sunny Sundays do we get? And watching a rugby match is one thing, but if you are not careful you will be roped in to make the teas and wash the strip as well.

However, far more dangerous, in my view, are the kind of hobbies that seem innocuous – particularly those which can be done at home and therefore pursued at all hours of the day and night. Not many girls like to think their charms would fade into insignificance when compared to the attractions of a home computer. But believe me, it can happen. At least with rugby, football, cricket and other sports you can become involved in some way or another if you want to – even if it is only meeting to congratulate or commiserate in the pub afterwards. But the one-to-one relationships some men have with their computers are impossible to crack.

**Where to meet men**

A study carried out in 1970 showed that most couples met at a dance, a party or at work, in that order. More recent surveys confirm that things have not changed very much, only these days for dance, read disco. But what if you do not have a girl friend to go to discos with, if no one you know throws parties and you work in an all-female environment like a nursery school or a shop?

Do not despair. There are other ways of meeting men. There are dating agencies, contact clubs and classified ads, to start with.

**Dating agencies**
Probably the best known agency is Dateline, which has been going since 1966 and uses a computer to bring men and women together. There are currently around 35,000 members spread all over the country. Over the age range (eighteen to seventy) there are more men than women; the majority of members are aged under thirty;

a steadily growing sector is the second time around single person.

In the middle of 1983 (the most up-to-date figures) the men listed on the computer files were as follows:

| | |
|---|---:|
| 25 years or younger | 5,811 |
| 26–35 | 7,860 |
| 36–45 | 3,142 |
| 46–55 | 1,286 |
| 56–65 | 458 |

Of these, 75 per cent were single, 3 per cent widowers, 8 per cent separated and 14 per cent divorced.

To join Dateline you fill in a five-page questionnaire giving information about yourself, the kind of people you want to meet, your personality, your relationships, your lifestyle, your work and your interests and activities. It normally costs £75 for a year's membership although there are special rates for certain groups – if you are a woman under twenty the fee is £35, under twenty-five, £45.

So what do you get for your money? Once your details have been fed into the computer it will search its memory to find compatible men to introduce you to. You will then be sent a list of up to six names and addresses and it is up to you to make contact. If you want the computer to try again, each run costs a further £2. You can pay for as many extra runs as you like. If you get fewer than three names on any run you get a free go. At the same time as the computer is checking its files to send you your list, it is putting your details into its memory so that it can send out your name to interested and compatible men. So you may be phoned by men who have been given your name as a contact.

Does it work? Pauline Chandler of Dateline says:

> If you assess success in terms of marriage/steady relationships, then I can tell you that I get letters from almost 1,000 people a year asking to be taken off the system because they have met someone through the service. In addition to those people there are those, of course, who quietly meet, stop using the service and never let us know what has happened.
>
> I won't pretend we don't get complaints; we do, and we

have a member of staff who spends her whole time dealing with queries and complaints. The vast majority can be resolved and where we can't help someone then we refund their fee.

Dateline is by no means the only dating agency – if you want one that operates locally, it is worth checking the classified columns of your local paper or looking in magazines like *Time Out*.

## Contact clubs

You can usually find these advertising for members in the same kind of places. They are not really lonely hearts clubs – although a fair number of lonely people join them – but aim, instead, to provide people with a choice of different events where they can have fun and make new friends at the same time. The members themselves usually organize and hold the events and so the kind of things on offer can vary enormously depending on the imagination, energy and enthusiasm of members at any one time. It is probably best to look for an organization which offers quite a large choice. As one girl friend of mine put it:

You soon get tired of going to wine and cheese parties, pub evenings and parties and going over the same old questions all the time. 'Why did you join?' 'Where do you work?' 'Where do you live?' and so on. It's much better if you can go out to a theatre in a group, or round an exhibition – at least you have something else to talk about.

The clubs can also help if you are keen on some kind of sport but do not want to join a particular place on your own – many arrange swimming parties, squash evenings, badminton games. Or bridge, horseriding, skating – the list is pretty extensive and once you are a member it may be possible to find fellow enthusiasts by organizing events yourself.

Most of the clubs run introductory nights, often held in a particular pub or hotel where you can meet some of the members and be given some of the basic information. There is usually some kind of age limit, but the upper and lower limits vary.

In London, for example, Breakaway (membership is open only to professional, well-dressed/mannered single people) set the limits between twenty-three and forty-five. You can get a free one week's trial membership. Thereafter, it costs from £5 a month.

The IVC Club has its own premises in London's Covent Garden where it holds its introductory evenings. The annual subscription is £42 a year (there is also a £2 joining fee). The age range is from eighteen to forty. Like most of these kind of clubs, what you get for your money is a monthly magazine, listing all the events on offer. You then choose the ones you fancy. Some, like concerts or weekend house parties, have to be booked in advance. Others, you can simply turn up to. Extra charges for each event vary, but generally the aim is simply to cover the costs whether it is the price of a theatre ticket or a bottle of wine.

### Lonely hearts ads

Lots of publications from *Private Eye* to the *Spectator* carry 'lonely hearts' ads. You can either place one of your own (in which case it is probably best to seek refuge behind a Box number) or answer one of the ads already in print.

The choice is pretty wide – but it pays to be cynical. Anyone who says he is seeking a 'warm, loving relationship' or a 'sensuous, vivacious woman to entertain during the daytime as evening work prevents normal contact' is probably after no strings sex or is married. (And these quotes came from genuine ads.)

The same goes for all those 'company directors' seeking a 'fun-loving, attractive girlfriend' or 'busty, lusty lady'. And as for those men who sound too good to be true, no doubt they are.

On the other hand, if you do decide to sit down and draw up your own ad, you will soon realize how hard it can be. Do you go for the humorous approach? 'Frozen, fat, forty (tall brunette) needs large, warm male to thaw her out . . .' Or the artistic approach? 'Juliet seeks Romeo . . .'

It is not easy trying to sum up your own personality and your requirements in the space of a few lines. Nor is it particularly cheap. The 'CARING female, 33, tall, slim, aware' who 'enjoys books, arts, communicating, muddy wellies, hugs and more' and was seeking a 'loving male counterpart' through the columns of *Time Out*, for instance, would have spent £20.10 on her four-line ad, at the going rate of 70p a word (80p for capitals) and £4.00 for a Box Number.

Besides the classified columns of newspapers and magazines you can also find a good choice of lonely hearts ads in *Singles*, which, as its title suggests, is specifically aimed at the single market. This monthly magazine, produced by the same organization which runs the Dateline computer dating service, costs 75p and is available from W. H. Smith, Menzies and other newsagents. To advertise yourself costs £10 for twenty words, and 30p a word thereafter. Box numbers are an extra £1, semi-display ads an extra £5 and photographs an extra £15.

## Nexus

One organization which seems to cross the dividing lines between the dating agencies, the contact clubs and the lonely hearts columns is Nexus, which describes itself as a 'communications service'. Be that as it may, it does offer a variety of ways to meet other people. For a fee of £61.20 a year or £42.60 for six months (and then for a renewal fee of £36 a year) you get a membership card which entitles you to use a number of different services.

You get a monthly bulletin, telling you about the events which are being organized by other members and which you can attend. You also get a folio of 'icebreakers' – short accounts, written by new members, explaining why they have joined and asking people to get in touch with them.

You have access to what Nexus call the Leisure Directory, which lists people in terms of their interests. So if you want to find someone to share your interest in hang gliding or stamp collecting, and who lives reasonably close to you, this is one way to do it.

Another way of making new friends is to offer your services to the Skill Bank. This sends out regular bulletins to members and enables people to meet because they can offer help to each other. For instance, some people say they type, others offer gardening or DIY skills. This way, not only can you make new friends by giving your time and energy, but you make friends who can help you in return.

There is also an International register which will put you in touch with Nexus members abroad and give you the chance of playing hostess to visitors to Britain. And, finally, there is the tape service, another variation on the blind date. By ringing a particular phone number you can listen to other Nexus members talking about themselves and decide whether any of them would be interesting to meet. You then contact the office for their name and phone number.

In August 1983 *Which?*, the magazine of the Consumers' Association, looked at marriage bureaux and dating services. They warned that:

—one in three people in their survey who had used an agency was dissatisfied,

—not all contacts are genuine; two out of four offered to one woman were married men looking for an affair,

—you could end up spending a lot of money – but lonely hearts ads worked out cheaper and two out of three people who had tried them thought they were worthwhile.

Although some marriage bureaux or dating agencies may belong to an association – such as the Association of British Introduction Agencies or the Society of Marriage Bureaux, each with its own code of practice – neither of these is fully endorsed by the Office of Fair Trading and there are no specific controls over people who want to set up in business for themselves.

*Which?* suggested that if you planned to use a bureau or agency you should be your own watchdog. Before you part with your money you should ask specifically:

—Is it a marriage bureau or a dating service? Must members be free to marry and, if so, must they sign something to that effect?

—How do they keep information confidential, and what do they tell prospective partners?

—How many clients do they have in your age range and area? Realistically, how many contacts are you likely to get?

—How closely will these contacts match your description?

—How do you go about getting more contacts if the first are unsuitable?

—How are meetings arranged? Are both parties consulted first or are names and addresses handed out for you to contact the others?

—What are the fees and what do they cover?

—How are complaints handled – money back or membership extended?

Another avenue worth checking out is your local Trading Standards Office, to see if they have received any complaints.

In the end, *Which?* concluded, you have to go into the whole business in the right frame of mind. 'Treat it as a gamble, don't expect to win and if hearts come up trumps, then congratulations. You can be lucky and make a good match.'

Being in the right frame of mind is the key to man-meeting. After all, you can try every evening class from aerobics to zoo-keeping, go on three singles holidays a year, prop up the corner seat in the wine bar every evening and it will not make a blind bit of difference if you are giving off the wrong kind of vibrations. Whether you freeze men out with your shyness or frighten them off with your eagerness to please, you alone can do something about it.

One tip is to stop doing things because you hope to find a man that way, but to do them for yourself. Who knows – if you start to study local history because it fascinates you, romance may blossom at the library. The more things you are interested in, the more interesting you will be to others – and that includes men.

And – even if you do think you have found Mr Right – never neglect your girl friends. As one single girl says:

You never know when you will need them. If things do go wrong they can be your way back on to the social scene. After all, the men they know and the new men they meet may not suit them.

But it's a bit like throwing a pebble into a pond. The ripples spread. Through your girl friends you can meet people they work with, went to school with, live next door to. And through those people you can meet others. And some of those will be eligible men. And one of those may be Superman!

## Useful addresses and telephone numbers

Dateline:   23 Abingdon Road, London W8, 01-938 1011.

Breakaway: 01-991 2169

London Village: 01-586 7455 (24-hour information tape)

IVC: meetings every Wednesday from 7 pm to 9 pm at the Intervarsity Club, 3-5 The Piazza, corner of James Street and King Street Covent Garden, London WC2, 01-240 2525.

Nexus: Head office, 01-359 7656 or 6703
    Scottish office, 041-221 1090
    Northern office, 061-834 8964
    Bristol office, 0454 321836
    Leeds office, 0532 445186
    Southern office, 0273 775578
    Midlands office, 0869 38801

# 5
# The Single Woman and The Law

There are times in every single woman's life when she needs a lawyer. Not necessarily the Rumpole of the Bailey crusading barrister to get her off a charge of shoplifting or drunken driving, but, more likely, one of the other kind: a solicitor.

You might, if you are one of the countless women facing the single state again, need a solicitor to help you with a divorce. You might want a solicitor to help you draw up a will. You might need a solicitor to help you buy a house or flat.

Few of us have a firm of family lawyers handy, so how do you go about finding someone to act for you? The first thing to realize is that certain firms specialize in certain types of work. So your nearest High Street solicitor's office may be just the place to go if you want someone to handle the conveyancing on your home-buying deal, but not necessarily the best firm for seeing you through your divorce.

The best way of finding a solicitor is through personal recommendation, but failing that you can always try your local Citizens' Advice Bureau. They will not recommend anyone in particular, but they can often point you in the direction of firms with experience in the type of problem you have. They should have a copy of the Solicitors' Regional Directory, which names solicitors in England and Wales and tells you broadly the experience of each. They should also have a list of firms who work under the Legal Aid scheme and even if you do not qualify for help under the scheme (see p.87), you can check the list for details of the kind of work each law firm does. This list – and the directory – is also available at libraries.

Many inner city areas have neighbourhood law centres and these can often give free help with some problems, such as difficulties with landlords or tenants. And if they cannot help, they can usually recommend a solicitor in private practice. The Law Centres' Federation is the place to contact if you do not know of a law centre near you. You can also check in the local phone directory.

Of course, if you have the time and energy – or, perhaps, more importantly, if you do not have the money – you can act as your own lawyer over certain matters. The numbers of people conducting their own divorces, for instance, are rising steadily. The Consumers' Association publishes a useful book called *Getting A Divorce* and you can also get a booklet called *Undefended Divorce* from the Divorce Registry or your local county court which tells you how to go about things. However, if your case is anything but straightforward, it is probably in your best interests to see a solicitor.

Similarly, you can handle your own conveyancing when you are buying a house or flat. Once again, the Consumers' Association has published a book which takes you step by step through the process. It is called *The Legal Side of Buying a House*.

Lots of single women never think of making a will – it is something we all seem to be a little superstitious about. And if all your worldly goods can be packed into the back of a dilapidated Mini, then there is probably little point. On the other hand, once you own property, it may well be worth thinking about those you would like to be your inheritors should you suddenly join the ranks of the dear departed.

For people who die without making a will, the law lays down rules for the way their estate should be divided up. If you are single, have never married and have no children, for instance, everything goes to your parents or if you have no parents, to your brothers and sisters and so on through other relatives. If there are no relatives, the Crown gets the lot.

You can buy ready printed forms for wills at stationery shops and if your situation is fairly simple, there is no reason why you should not write your own, using one of these forms. The Consumers' Association also publishes a book called *Wills and Probate*, which explains how to prepare a will, sign it and have it witnessed. However, if there are any complications in your life – an ex-husband, children, a man you are living with and who you want to inherit your stereo and potted plants as well as the two-up, two-down you have lovingly restored to its former glory together – once again it is probably best to get your will drawn up by an expert. There is a saying that solicitors like nothing better than wills people have drawn up themselves!

Going to see a solicitor need not cost the earth. As mentioned earlier, neighbourhood law centres may be able to give some advice free and a number of lawyers operate a special scheme which allows you to have a fixed-fee interview. This allows anyone – whatever their financial status – to have half an hour of a solicitor's time for £5. This is usually enough time for you to explain your problem and get some idea of the possible courses of action. Not all firms of solicitors offer this service, but most do.

If you earn very little and have few savings you may be entitled to free legal help, or you may only have to pay a contribution towards the cost of your solicitor's charges. The financial limits change from time to time to take account of inflation but your local Citizens' Advice Bureau should have up-to-date figures and leaflets explaining how the scheme works, and they will help you find out whether or not you qualify.

Briefly, the scheme is in two parts: 'legal advice and assistance' (usually known as the green form scheme) and legal aid proper. If you qualify under the green form scheme you can get help and advice from a solicitor on almost any legal problem, either free or partly free. This help may include explaining your rights, writing letters for you, filling in forms, making a will or preparing a case for a tribunal.

Legal aid itself is money to cover all or part of the cost of having a solicitor to represent you in court, either in a civil or a criminal case.

## Driving and the law

Most of us hope we will go through life never having to appear in any kind of court. In fact, there are a number of ways in which we may fall foul of the law. If you own and drive a car, for instance, can you honestly put your hand on your heart and swear that you have never, ever broken the law? Do you even know the penalties for which you are liable? The AA motoring organization publishes a leaflet called *The Law About Penalties* which gives some information as to the maximum fines for the most common motoring offences. It makes sobering reading. Here are some examples:

| Offence | Punishment | Disqualification | Endorsement | Penalty Points |
|---|---|---|---|---|
| Speeding | £200 | Discretionary | Obligatory | 3 |
| Using or keeping a vehicle without an excise licence | £200 or five times the duty payable | – | – | – |
| Failing to stop after an accident | £1,000 | Discretionary | Obligatory | 5-9 |
| Inconsiderate driving | £500 | Discretionary | Obligatory | 2-5 |
| Driving or attempting to drive with blood alcohol concentration above prescribed limit | £1,000 or six months or both | Obligatory | Obligatory | |

Besides this leaflet, the AA publishes a number of others designed to cover the topics of law raised most frequently by members. If you belong to the AA these are available from your Regional HQ or any AA centre. They cover such topics as speed limits, lights, seat belts, parking at night, drinking and driving.

The AA also provides members with free legal advice on problems they consider may arise directly from the use or ownership of a motor vehicle. They may also be able to help negotiate a satisfactory settlement in cases involving disputes with garages, car dealers and so on. And they may pay the fees for a solicitor of their choice to represent a member being prosecuted for a motoring offence, whether or not she is pleading guilty.

To find out about the services available you should phone or write to your Regional HQ. It is no good joining after the event, however – all these services apply only to members who have paid the appropriate subscription *before* the alleged incident.

If you are a driver involved in an accident, the law says there are a number of steps you must take. (An accident is said to have occurred if a person is injured, other than you as the driver; damage is caused to another vehicle; damage is caused to an animal, other than one in or on your vehicle or trailer; or damage is caused to property.)

In any of these circumstances you MUST:

1. Stop and remain at the scene for a reasonable period.

2. Give your name, address (and those of the owner of the vehicle if it is not yours) and registration number to anyone with reasonable grounds who asks for it,

   OR, if details are not exchanged at the scene of an accident, report the accident at a police station or to a police officer as soon as reasonably practicable and in any case within twenty-four hours. (A phone call is not good enough.)

In addition, if anyone else is injured you MUST:

1. Produce your certificate of insurance to anyone with reasonable grounds who asks for it,

   OR, if the certificate is not produced at the scene, report the accident at a police station or to a police officer as soon as possible and in any case, within twenty-four hours, and produce your certificate of insurance.

2. If you cannot produce your certificate when you report the accident to the police, you have five days to take it to any police station you specify when you originally report the accident.

Apart from this, of course, you should report all accidents to your insurance company. Shock sets in even after very minor bumps, but do try to keep cool if you are involved in a car smash of any kind and try to make a note of what happened as soon as possible afterwards. This will help you not only when it comes to completing your insurer's accident report form, but also in case of any further legal proceedings.

Try to get names and addresses of independent witnesses as well as the name and address of any other driver involved, and the name and address of whoever owns the vehicle or vehicles if these differ. You also ought to get the name and address of the other people's insurance company and the registration number of the vehicle. (Check this against the tax disc.) If the police were called, you should record the officer's number.

You should also try to set down the damage caused, the date, time and location of the accident, the speed of the vehicles involved, the width of the road, road markings and signs, conditions of the road surface and the state of the weather. Are there any relevant marks or debris on the road? What was the other party's driving like? Were the other driver and any front passenger wearing seat belts? (Failure to wear seat belt has been regarded by the Courts as a ground for reducing damages awarded for personal injuries by up to a quarter.)

What was visibility like? Did other vehicles have their lights on? Was the street lighting on? It often helps to make a rough sketch showing where the vehicles were before and after the accident – and if you happen to have a camera lurking in the glove compartment, photographs of the vehicles and the scene can be helpful.

## Your rights

Apart from having a brush with the law as a motorist, you may find yourself being stopped, questioned or even arrested by the police under other circumstances, so it pays to know your rights. The National Council for Civil Liberties publishes a number of fact sheets covering these eventualities. Usually, when the police ask for your assistance you will want to help, but it may be in your own interests to know when you are not legally obliged to co-operate.

Since this is not a police state, neither the police nor anyone else has a *general* power to stop you, make you answer questions or take you to a police station without arresting you. But, in practice, there are quite a number of instances where some, or all, of these things could quite legally be done. For instance, the police can stop and search you in the streets if they have reasonable grounds to think you possess prohibited drugs, firearms, stolen goods (in some parts of the country) or anything connected with terrorism. They can ask you for your name and address if:

—you are driving a motor vehicle,
—you are suspected of creating a disturbance at a public meeting,
—you are suspected of possessing prohibited drugs,
—you are suspected of having an offensive weapon in a public place,
—you fail to produce a ticket or pay the fare on a train,
—you possess a firearm and fail to produce a firearms certificate.

Sometimes the police ask people to go to a police station to 'help them with their enquiries'. You should ask if you are being arrested. If the answer is 'no', then in theory you can choose whether to go or not. In practice, if you refuse you may find yourself arrested anyway.

The NCCL suggest that if you go voluntarily to the station you should get a solicitor or some other independent person to go with you. They say: 'Although you have the right to contact a friend or lawyer once you get to the station, this is usually difficult.'

Normally, police need a warrant from a magistrates' court to arrest someone. But there are cases where a warrant is not required:

—when a police officer has reasonable cause to suspect you have committed, are committing or are about to commit an arrestable offence (usually one carrying at least a five-year maximum prison sentence),

—when it is necessary to prevent or stop a breach of the peace,
—when it is reasonable to suspect you are obstructing the highway,
—if you are suspected of possessing an offensive weapon,
—if you refuse to take or fail to pass a breathalyser,
—if you are found drunk and incapable in a public place.

As you see, these cover a variety of scenarios from theft to demonstrations, pub brawls to drunk driving.

If you are arrested without a warrant the police should take you to a magistrates' court within twenty-four hours, or forty-eight hours at weekends; or release you on bail. They should also caution you that anything you say may be put down in writing and used as evidence. They should tell you as soon as possible the offences you are to be charged with, and they should allow you to contact by phone or telegram your family, a friend or a lawyer. Fuller details are given in the NCCL fact sheet on 'Arrest'.

The NCCL advise anyone who is arrested to go quietly. They say:

> Always try to remain polite and reasonable. If you have been arrested wrongly or deprived of your rights, you may be able to sue for false imprisonment or assault, or make a complaint against the police, later.
>
> In general, don't make any statement or answer questions until you've had legal advice. Beware of any inducement or threat. Pleading guilty in return for an offer of bail can harm your case.

### Disturbances

Besides knowing what your rights are and how to behave if you seem temporarily on the wrong side of the law, there may be times when you need to know how to make the law work for you.

Calling the police is not necessarily the best thing to do. For instance, if you are being driven mad by noisy neighbours, the police may be reluctant to become embroiled in what is basically a civil matter. So what *should* you do if the man next door seems to be dismantling his house brick by brick and rebuilding it in the early hours of each morning, or if the students whose flat is over yours seem addicted to constant all-night rock parties?

Assuming you have already had a face-to-face meeting with your noisy neighbour, explained how difficult they are making life for you and asked them to keep the noise down to a reasonable level at reasonable times of the day, and got nowhere, the next step is to start keeping a record.

If you are just worried by the odd disturbed night, the occasional rowdy party, you can probably do little. But if there is a constant nuisance and your health is suffering, you may be able to get the Environmental Health Officer (who works for the local authority) to take some action. It will help your case if you have some kind of noise log to show him and if you can get other neighbours to complain with you. Initially, the Environmental Health Officer may try to sort the situation out amicably, but, if all else fails, he may resort to the courts to get the noise stopped.

Disturbing though noisy neighbours can be, coping with obscene phone callers can be even more distressing. But, once again, contacting the police is not the only thing you can do to stop the nuisance. It is an offence to use the phone for making offensive, indecent or menacing calls – or to use the phone to cause annoyance or anxiety and British Telecom will help obtain evidence for the police. But they also give advice to women who may find themselves being pestered in this way. They suggest hanging up without responding in any way as soon as you become aware that a call is dodgy. Other women's groups suggest keeping a whistle by the phone to blow very loudly in order to discourage obscene callers. Some women say it works if you pretend you cannot make out what the caller is saying. ('You've got a twelve inch what?'). However, many psychologists feel that men who make these kind of calls get their kicks from the reactions of the caller, whatever they are.

Even if the calls persist, if you do not react at all the caller will get fed up with the lack of response and give up.

If you live alone, though, it can be very upsetting to be plagued by calls of this kind. It makes sense not to advertise the fact that you are female by having only your initials and surname listed in the phone directory and British Telecom also suggest that you do not give your name, address or number to strangers who phone. If they ask for your number, they say, you should simply ask them what number they dialled.

You can always contact the customer services manager of your local phone area for advice. In some areas it may be possible to have all your calls intercepted by the operator for no extra charge. This can cause delays for genuine callers trying to ring you, but this may also discourage the nuisance caller, who will not appreciate being asked the number he has dialled and his own name and number.

You can change your number altogether (this costs £11) or go ex-directory. This either means being completely unlisted, and with the operator giving no information to callers (genuine or otherwise) who do not have your number; not being listed in the phone book, but with directory enquiries having your number to give to callers; not being listed but with directory inquiries being prepared to offer calls to you. It is then up to you whether you accept a particular call or not. The first two services are free, while the third costs £12.50 plus VAT per quarter and is added to your rental charges.

As a last resort you could have all incoming calls barred, although this would obviously cut down the usefulness of having a phone in the first place. And you might have to pay a 'nominal' fee for this.

British Telecom say they never initiate the tracing of nuisance calls, but if the police are notified and start investigations, they will try to help – and, they say, the police do regularly and successfully prosecute offenders. But one of the first things you must do if you are going to contact the police is to keep a record of all nuisance calls, trying to note any information which may be useful, such as background noises, type of voice, whether or not the call was made from a call box and so on.

## Useful addresses and publications

The Law Centres Federation:   Duchess House, 18-19 Warren Street, London, W1P 5DB, 01-387 8570.

The Consumers' Association:   14 Buckingham Street, London WC2, 01-839 1222.

The Divorce Registry:   Somerset House, Strand, London WC2, 01-405 7641

The Automobile Association:   Head Office, Fanum House, Basingstoke, Hampshire, 0256 20123.

The National Council for Civil Liberties:   21 Tabard Street, London SE1, 01-403 3888.

British Telecom publishes a leaflet called 'Nuisance Callers', which is available from your local sales office (ask the operator to put you through).

The *Penguin Guide to Civil Liberties* is currently out of print but may be available through your library.

*The Solicitors' Regional Directory*, produced by the Law Society, is available at local libraries, advice centres and similar offices.

# 6
# The Single Woman at the Shops

The popular image of the single woman at the shops is one of a person in her element, gaily frittering away time and money in the pursuit of an occupation she finds supremely satisfying. In fact, most surveys show that women – single or not – tend to find shopping a chore, whether it is for food, goods or clothes.

Shopping expeditions can be bad enough when you have to run the gauntlet of disinterested shop assistants who tend to answer all queries with unhelpful statements such as 'If it's not on display we haven't got it', or 'we get deliveries on Thursdays; we may get some more in then. You will have to pop in and see.' Add to these charmers the delights of ploughing through racks of garments in the vain hope of finding your size (self-service sometimes feels like another name for masochism) and then queuing for ages to pay because only one check-out is operating, and it becomes clear why shopping is just as likely to be stressful rather than soothing.

## The Sale of Goods Act

What is worse is that sinking feeling when you get home only to discover that the dress the salesgirl swore was handwashable is not; the non-stick pans do stick and the record of your favourite singer is so scratched you cannot play it.

In England and Wales the law has three rules when it comes to the sale of goods. (The Office of Fair Trading publishes a leaflet explaining these and also two leaflets explaining the law in Scotland and Northern Ireland.)

Under the Sale of Goods Act 1979:

1. Whatever you buy must be of *merchantable quality*. In other words, they must be reasonably fit for their normal purpose. New items should not be broken or damaged and should work properly, although you cannot expect goods which are very cheap, secondhand or 'seconds' to be of top quality.

2. The goods must be *as described* – whether this is by the sales staff, the packaging or the display sign in the shop. In other words, a polyester mix blouse should not be sold as cotton, plastic shoes as leather, for example.

3. The goods must be *fit for any particular purpose* made known to the seller. In other words, if you explain to the assistant you want some shoes to go jogging in, she should not sell you 'fashion' shoes which will fall apart after one spin round the block.

So what should you do if you think you have a case? First of all, remember that prevention is better than cure. However rushed you are, it does pay to examine whatever you intend to buy carefully before you part with your cash. Next, make sure you keep receipts. It is all too easy to lose those tiny scraps of paper so it may be an idea to keep a folder at home specially for them and simply file each one away at the end of a shopping trip. Every six months or so you can have a clear-out.

If something is wrong with your purchase then you should stop using it at once and contact the shop or company where you bought it. (If you were given the item as a present, then whoever bought it for you has to make the claim.) Take the goods back to the shop and ask to see the manager. It may help to phone first to make sure he or she will be there when you go.

Do not lose your temper – not at first, anyway. You want the manager to be sympathetic, not hostile, and if you go storming in like Attila the Hun, you are far more likely to put everyone's backs up than to get the fair deal you deserve. On the other hand, do not be apologetic. Remind yourself that YOU are not the one at fault.

Make up your mind what you want BEFORE you go – and stick to it, firmly but politely. Take your receipt or proof of purchase if you can.

If any of the three rules have been broken you can *either* get a cash payment to make up the difference between what you have paid and the reduced value of the faulty item, *or* you can reject it and get your money back.

If you *both* agree you may have a replacement or a free repair. You do not have to accept a credit note. If you do and cannot find anything else you want, it may not be easy to get your money back later.

Exactly what you are entitled to depends on how serious the fault is, and how soon you tell the seller. If you buy a pair of shoes one day and the heel comes off the next, you have a much stronger case than if you buy a pair of shoes, wear them for three months and then take them back because the stitching is fraying.

And you are not entitled to anything if you:

—examined the item when you bought it and should have seen the faults,
—were told about the faults,
—simply change your mind about wanting it,
—did the damage yourself.

If the local shop or office where you go to make your initial complaint cannot or will not help, contact the managing director at the head office. Find out his name before you ring or write.

Find out if the firm belongs to a trade association. Some associations will intervene in disputes and those who have drawn up Codes of Practice have a special system for dealing with complaints. Many shoe shops, for instance, now display signs saying 'We honour the Code of Practice for Footwear'.

So, if you have a complaint about shoes bought from a shop covered by the Footwear Code, there are several ways of putting the matter right. You can either settle the matter with the manager of the shop. If he does not agree that your complaint is justified, he may – if you agree – offer to send them back to the manufacturer or to his head office for an opinion. (But remember, this should not be a way of passing the buck. If the shoes are faulty, it is the *retailer's*, not the manufacturer's, responsibility to put the matter right.)

If you are still not satisfied, either you or the shop can approach one of your local consumer advisers – the local authority Trading Standards or Consumer Protection department, the Citizens' Advice Bureau or Consumer Advice Centre, for their help in settling the matter. Alternatively, you can ask for the shoes to be sent to the Footwear Testing Centre for an independent report. There is a small charge for this – the shop pays two-thirds and you pay a third. But if your complaint is upheld, the retailer will refund your share. And he must abide by the findings of the report.

Apart from shoes, other areas covered by Codes of Practice include cars (both buying and servicing), electrical goods, furniture, film processing and photography, and launderers and dry cleaners. So if you are thinking of buying a car, a washing machine or a radio, a new sofa, having your holiday snaps printed or getting your best party dress cleaned, it may pay you to seek out a shop which has a notice on display telling you they will follow the Code.

If the shop you are at loggerheads with does not have a Code of Practice, however, and is not a member of a trade association who can you turn to for help?

**Citizens' Advice Bureaux**
Check the phone book for one in your area. They can help you complain successfully and advise you on your rights.

**Trading Standards or Consumer Protection departments**
These are local authority departments which investigate false or misleading descriptions or prices, inaccurate weights and measures, and some aspects of the safety of goods. Some areas have advice centres close to shopping areas, which give advice and deal with problems and complaints.

**Environmental Health departments**
These are also local authority departments which deal with health matters such as unfit food and drink, dirty shops and restaurants.

**Consumer groups**
In some areas local people form their own consumer groups to keep an eye on shopping problems. Check your library to see if there is one near you.

Sometimes a complaint is fairly straightforward – a matter of returning with a faulty item and asking for your money back. But sometimes a shop can try to hide behind notices which say 'No refunds' or by pointing out that the item you bought was 'in a sale' so you cannot expect to change it. The fact is that any notices which say 'no refunds' are illegal, even for sale goods. A trader cannot wriggle out of his responsibility if he sells you faulty goods. And all goods, whether bought in a sale or not, are covered if bought from a trader, i.e. from a shop, a street market, a door-to-door salesman or a mail order company.

Nor can shopkeepers refuse to consider a complaint simply because a guarantee has run out. Guarantees are worth reading carefully – they may be a useful bonus, or they may not cover everything. But, whatever a guarantee says, when something goes wrong you can still claim your rights from the shop.

It it also worth knowing that sometimes not only may you be able to claim your money back, but you may also be able to claim extra compensation if you have suffered a loss because of a faulty buy – if an iron that proves not to work properly burns your clothes, for instance. But this is the kind of situation where it might be a good idea to seek advice first from one of the bodies named above.

Thinking twice before you buy is always a good policy. But never more so than when it comes to large items which have to be ordered or on which you have to leave a deposit, or sign some kind of hire purchase or credit agreement.

It is all too easy to change your mind – only to realize, too late, that you are committed. When you agree to buy something, whether or not you pay any money at the time, you are making a contract with the seller.

This could be a written contract (when you sign an order form, for example), or a verbal agreement as simple as asking your local hardware shop to order you a food mixer. And if you change your mind and try to break the contract, not only could you lose any deposit you might have paid, you could also be sued for more money up to the full price of the goods or services ordered. This is why it is vital that you and the seller are absolutely clear as to what is being agreed. If you are asked to sign a form or agreement, always read it through, however tedious it seems, and even if the salesman tells you it is 'just the standard form'.

Under certain circumstances, however, it may be possible to get your money back. Sometimes a trader will agree, when you place an order, that you can have your deposit back if you later decide not to go ahead. If so, it may save problems later to get this in writing.

If the goods, when they arrive, are faulty under the terms of the Sale of Goods Act (as defined on p.96) you need not accept them and can claim your money back.

Also, if the shop does not keep its side of the bargain by being unable to supply the model, size or colour you ordered, for instance, or by being unable to deliver on time, you would have a case.

When ordering something it is always best to specify a date for delivery, so that if the goods are not delivered on time you can cancel the order and get your money back. Even if you have not specified a date you can allow a reasonable time, then contact the seller and say that if you do not receive the goods by a certain date (say, within 14 days) you will no longer require them and will want your money back.

Since 1983 the protection for consumers provided by the Sale of Goods Act has been extended to cover goods supplied as part of a service, on hire or in part exchange. In other words, if you have taps fitted by a plumber, if you hire a ladder to do some decorating, or if you get a new gas cooker by trading in your old one, in all these cases the goods must be of 'merchantable quality', 'fit for the purpose' and 'as described'. So the taps should not leak; the ladder should be long enough for the ceilings you said you had to paint; and the cooker should not be described as having an automatic pilot if you have to use matches to light it.

In addition, since July 1983, the law dealing with the standard of services – such as those provided by builders, plumbers, TV repairers, hairdressers and garages – has been tidied up. Unless anything more specific is agreed between you and the person supplying the service, he or she must now do so:

1. with reasonable care and skill,
2. within a reasonable time,
3. for a reasonable charge.

What is considered 'reasonable' is decided by comparing a job with the 'normal' standard for providing that particular service. And if a supplier does not observe all three of these conditions, you may be entitled to claim some or all of your money back.

If you have a complaint and you cannot sort this out with the TV repair man, the Electricity Board or whoever, you can seek advice from the various bodies mentioned on p.99 who specialize in consumer problems.

Public services – such as gas, electricity, postal and telephone services and British Rail – have their own consumer or consultative councils and some companies will belong to trade associations. These may be your next port of call.

Finally, whether you have a complaint about the service or the goods provided by someone, you may end up considering legal action. But do take advice first.

In the past, if all efforts to settle a consumer problem amicably failed, many women simply gave up because they were unable to afford the risk of going to court and having to pay legal costs. On top of this, court procedure can be rather overwhelming.

However, court procedure has now been simplified so that it is possible to bring small claims – usually up to £500 – before the courts without knowing anything much about the law and without having to pay to be legally represented.

These informal 'small claims courts' operate as part of the county court system, and are only concerned with private disputes, not criminal cases. Many of the claims fall into the following classes:

—claims for payments of debts – perhaps for goods sold, work done or money lent,

—claims arising out of the sale of goods, including repairing damaged goods, failure to supply goods ordered or supplying the wrong article or a defective one,

—claims against people providing consumer services – garages, dry cleaners, electrical repairers etc. – in respect of faulty workmanship or failure to do the work that was agreed.

For these 'small' claims the hearing usually takes place before an arbitrator, generally in private, without the formalities associated with a trial. The aim is to enable people to have small disputes resolved in an informal atmosphere and since the formalities are kept to a minimum, you should have no difficulty in handling your own case.

Full details on how to sue and defend actions without a solicitor are contained in the booklet *Small Claims in the County Court*, available from the Lord Chancellor's Office or your local county court. The Consumers' Association also publishes a book called *How to Sue in the County Court*. And, once again, citizens' advice bureaux would be able to give you advice.

## Credit

Sorting out problems when things you buy or services you receive from shops and traders go wrong is just one of the headaches a single woman may have to face. Another area which can be a minefield is that of consumer credit. Under the Sex Discrimination Act, women must now be offered credit on the same terms as men. So, if you want a loan to buy something on hire purchase you may be asked for a guarantor, or you may be turned down as a 'bad risk' – but ONLY if the same rules are applied to men.

If you think you have been discriminated against because you are a woman, you can contact the Equal Opportunities Commission. It can tell you about your rights and intervene on your behalf if necessary. It can also help you decide whether you have grounds for legal action under the Sex Discrimination Act and may be able to offer legal help or help with legal costs if you want to start a court case.

It can come as quite a shock to be turned down for credit on the grounds that you are a bad risk. Companies which provide credit facilities often use credit reference agencies which keep files on people to show whether or not they are likely to keep up payments. Since 1977 the Consumer Credit Act has given everyone the right to see their own credit reference file, check its accuracy and challenge it if it contains inaccurate or misleading information. Wrong information has led to people being unfairly refused credit.

So, when you apply to a company for credit you have a right to ask for the name and address of any credit reference agency they will be using. You can then contact the agency and for a nominal fee they must send you a copy of what is on your file. This is when you can amend your file – perhaps some of the information is wrong and you want it removed altogether. Perhaps you want to add a note explaining that you failed to keep up payments on a previous purchase because the goods were faulty.

The agency must let you know whether they have done as you wished or not and if you are still not happy with the result you can appeal to the Office of Fair Trading.

So much for getting credit – but what kind of credit is best? It is always worth shopping around before you commit yourself to any credit agreement. It may be better, for example, to get a personal loan from the bank than to arrange a hire purchase agreement through a store. Or perhaps opening a budget account with the store itself would suit you best of all.

One way of measuring one credit deal against another is to compare the APR – the 'annual percentage rate' of charge. Unlike most other rates used in the past, APR includes the interest on the loan itself and any other charges you may have to pay as a condition of getting the loan. Because credit traders must calculate APR according to standard formulae laid down by the Consumer Credit Act, you can use APR to compare one type of credit with another. In other words a credit deal with an APR of 29 per cent is a better deal than another, maybe quite different one, with an APR of 33 per cent.

But there are other factors you will need to consider.

These include:

—the cash price,
—the deposit (if any)
—the amount and the frequency of the repayments,
—the total amount payable,
—the period of the loan and whether the interest rate or any other charge can be varied during it,
—whether you will have to offer any security.

As an example you can see how a sofa, for instance, could be bought from a department store, using three different kinds of credit.

You could get *hire purchase* through the store, a *personal loan* from a bank or open a *budget account* with the store. Let us suppose the sofa cost £375.

*HP:* Cash price £375
To be repaid by 24 equal monthly instalments of £20.93
Total amount payable £502.32 (APR = 34.2 per cent)

*Loan:* Loan £375
To be repaid by 24 equal monthly instalments of £18.61
Total amount payable £446.64 (APR = 18.8 per cent)

*Budget account:* Opening a budget account can give you a credit limit which is usually a multiple the size of your monthly payment – say 24 times. So if you pay £20 a month, your limit is £480.

To clear the account will take 24 payments of £20 plus £8.88 from the 25th, because interest is charged each month on the outstanding balance.

Total amount payable £488.88 (APR = 29.8 per cent)

This example was taken from a leaflet called *The True Cost of Credit*, available from the Office of Fair Trading. They also produce another useful leaflet, *There's More to Credit Than Just HP.*

## Shoplifting

It is probably sensible in any discussion of shops and shopping to look at another area where your rights are involved, although, in this case, it is a matter of your rights as an individual, rather than as a consumer. You may be outraged to think that one day you could be accused of shoplifting, but it is worth knowing what might happen and how to cope with the situation.

People who campaign for a more sympathetic treatment for those accused of shoplifting often point out that shopping today in large stores, where you may have to travel fifty yards or more between picking up an item and getting to a check-out or till, give more opportunities for the mind to wander. They argue that it is all too easy to forget to pay something, without ever intending to steal.

My own view is that this kind of store, these kind of supermarkets, have been around long enough for us all to get used to them. We have all read stories about people putting tins of food into their shopping bag instead of the trolley 'by mistake', so we ought to be aware of the risks. However, the first lesson must be, when you are out shopping, particularly if you are in a rush or have other things on your mind, *stay alert*.

Keep your own shopping bags zipped up. Fold up your own carriers and keep them in a pocket until you need them – or get new ones each time. If you are a single mother who regularly goes shopping with a child, teach it not to touch things on counters or shelves and make it learn the lesson early on that items in shops – particularly things like sweets or crisps – have to be paid for before they become yours.

Most arrests for shoplifting are made by store detectives or managers. Because they are exercising their powers of a citizen's arrest (which are more limited than the police powers of arrest), they generally wait for someone to leave the store, as this is one way of their being able to say they had reasonable grounds to believe a person had committed an offence.

In fact, the detective or manager may not say they are arresting you. They may simply ask you to return to the store to answer some questions. If they *are* formally arresting you they must make this clear, and tell you the reason for your arrest.

If you do decide to go back voluntarily, bear in mind that you have no duty to answer anything they may ask you. In fact, you should be very careful what you say. If you are later charged with theft – and shoplifting is regarded as theft, not a separate, lesser crime – anything you say will almost certainly be repeated as evidence in court.

The National Council for Civil Liberties suggests that you co-operate as far as possible. Try not to get in a state and, if you can, say nothing except to deny any accusations, give a clear and positive explanation of how you paid for your goods and produce receipts. This is not always easy in the face of hostile questioning so it may be better to resort to some phrase such as 'I prefer not to say anything at this time'. Ask if you are free to go or whether you are being restrained. If you are not free to go you should be told you are under arrest and why, and you should be handed over to police custody as soon as possible.

The law relating to theft is very complicated and the prosecution has to prove a number of things to make the charge stick. So ask to see a solicitor or get legal advice and *do not* plead guilty unless you have done so. (Release provide a 24-hour emergency legal advice service if you do not have any other way of getting hold of a solicitor.)

Once you have been questioned by police officers, it may be weeks or months before you finally know whether you will have to appear in a magistrates' court to answer charges of theft. Police forces up and down the country vary in their ways of deciding whether or not to prosecute for first offence accusations of shoplifting, when the sums involved are fairly trivial.

Portia Trust North, an organization set up to help people accused of shoplifting, has produced a booklet which explains what happens from the time you are accused to your appearance in court. The Trust also offer support and counselling and practical help in the form of a 'McKenzie', someone who is not a lawyer but who can speak up for you in court. They can also supply, for your use as evidence, letters from people who walked out of stores without paying, realized their mistake and went back to pay up, as well as a copy of a report by a psychology professor on lapses of memory.

Another organization which offers befriending and counselling services is the Vincent Foundation, based in Stoke-on-Trent.

## Useful addresses and publications

Office of Fair Trading leaflets are obtainable free from consumer advice centres, many libraries and CABs. If you have trouble getting them locally, write to Room 310c, Office of Fair Trading, 15-25 Bream's Buildings, London EC4A 1PR. They include:
'How to Put Things Right' (England and Wales)
'Dear Shopper in Scotland'
'Dear Shopper in Northern Ireland'
'Stop and Think Before You Agree to Buy'
'No Credit?'

Release:   1 Elgin Avenue, London W9, 01-289 1123.

Portia Trust North: Emergency number: 01-603 8654. 15 Senhouse Street, Maryport, Cumbria, 0900 812114 (office hours), 0900 812379 (evenings, nights or weekends).
Leeds:   8-9 Albion Street, 0532 453983 or 0532 572961.
Gt. Yarmouth:   Mrs Valerie Balls, 61 Newnham Green, Gorleston-on-Sea, 0493 661599.
The Vincent Foundation: 9 Cheapside, Hanley, Stoke-on-Trent ST1 1HE, 0782 274652.

# 7

# The Single Woman and Her Money

Money may not buy you love but in this world it is essential for practically everything else. So it is no good burying your head in the sand, saying you have no head for figures and refusing to think about money matters. Today's single woman has to be able to do her sums.

Most single women over the age of eighteen have an income, either in the form of a student grant, a pay packet from an employer, or supplementary or unemployment benefit. Whatever form it takes, it affects the way you live, how much you can save and how much you can borrow.

## Tax

When you start work you receive a Tax Return form from the Inspector of Taxes which asks for details of your income and other personal commitments such as mortgage, life insurance, dependants. You have up to thirty days to fill in the form and return it to the Inspector who then sends you and your Employer a Notice of Coding, which gives you your tax code and provides a full breakdown showing how it was worked out.

Basically the system works like this. You earn a certain amount of money each year: at the same time you get 'allowances' – so that some of the money you earn is tax free and you are entitled to all of it. The rest of your income is taxable and, depending on the rates set by the Budget each year, you will pay a certain percentage of it in tax. You should automatically get a personal allowance for a single person but you will not get any of the other extra tax-free allowances unless you claim for them.

The Inspector usually sends you a tax return guide with the tax return form to help you fill it in. It lists the extra tax-free allowances you can claim, including fees or subscriptions to professional bodies, interest on loans, and an allowance for a child if you are a single mother.

Like most official forms, the Tax Return Guide looks rather daunting and if it really is beyond you, it is probably worth calling in at your local tax or enquiry office to ask for help. You will find this by looking under Inland Revenue in your local phone book. Alternatively, you may find the citizens' advice bureau can advise you.

Once you have been sent your Notice of Coding it is worth checking it (one survey showed that 25 per cent of all code numbers were incorrect.) If you think you are paying too much tax you will have to go back to the tax office which actually handles your file – and this will be the one that covers the area where you work, not the one for the area in which you live (unless, of course, the two are the same). Your employer should be able to give you the address.

When you change jobs your old employer should give you a form P45, which says how much you earned, how much tax you paid and what your tax code number is. If you give this to your new employer they should continue to deduct tax at the same rate as you were paying before.

If you have lost your P45, have still to get it from your previous employer, or if this is your first job, you will have tax deducted at the 'emergency' rate until you have filled in a tax return form. If you go down to a lower rate you will receive a tax rebate once you have been coded.

The way to check whether your code is right is to add up the tax allowances and reliefs you are entitled to and drop the last digit. If the allowances add up to £2,425, for example, the code would be 242. The letter after the code number shows the type of personal allowance you have – L stands for a lower rate of allowance, either the single person's allowance or the wife's earned income allowance; a single parent would have a code ending in H for a higher allowance.

When you receive your payslip you will notice that other deductions, besides tax, have been made. One of these will be for your National Insurance contributions. Before you leave school you are given a National Insurance number. If you do not know your number, ask your local social security office. Some of the benefits you are entitled to from the state depend on the NI contributions you pay.

If you are working – whether you are employed or self-employed – you have to pay NI contributions unless you earn less than an amount designated each year as the 'lower earnings limit'. There are four classes of contributions:

*Class 1:*  This is the most common if you work for someone else. (The employer also pays an additional contribution.) The amount you pay depends on your salary. (Leaflet NI 208 from the DHSS explains all.)

*Class 2:*  This is paid by the self-employed at a weekly flat rate. (Leaflet NI 41 and leaflet NI 27A).

*Class 3:*  These are voluntary contributions, paid weekly, by people such as students, women who are at home caring for dependants, and so on, to protect their pension rights. (Leaflet NI 42.)

Under certain circumstances you can be credited with contributions – if you are getting sickness benefit, for example, maternity allowance, or unemployment benefit. This should happen automatically, but if you have any doubts or, indeed, if you have any queries about NI, you should contact your local DHSS office.

*Class 4:*  These are paid by the self-employed in addition to Class 2, if profits exceed a certain amount. (Leaflet NP 18.)

When you open your pay packet or get your payslip you may have other deductions apart from tax and NI which make up the difference between your basic pay and your net pay (the money you actually receive). These might include a union subscription, a contribution to a private health insurance scheme, repayments for a loan made by your employer (to buy a season ticket, for example) or contributions into a company pension scheme.

## Banks and building societies

Some people prefer to be paid in cash but, according to National Westminster Bank, more than three-quarters of the working population have a bank account, so the chances are that your salary will be paid directly into a bank. If you do not want your money paid into a high street bank, however, you do not have to keep your hard-earned cash under the mattress.

You could put your money in the National Savings Bank, run by the Post Office. To open an account you simply go along to your local post office, fill in an application form and hand it in, with your money, at the counter.

The NSB pays interest on the balance in your account (with the first £70 a year tax free) but you do not get a cheque book. Instead, you can withdraw up to £100 cash on demand (although for amounts over £50 your bank book will normally be kept for checking). Larger amounts can be obtained within a few days by applying to the NSB in Glasgow and are paid either by crossed warrant, which is similar to a cheque, or in cash, by warrant payable at a named post office.

You can get regular payments of a fixed amount – for HP, mortgages, life insurance etc. – made by standing order from your NSB account. The Paybill service also allows you to pay bills, up to the total value of £250, which are normally payable at the post office, by filling in a withdrawal form for the total amount and presenting this at the post office counter along with the bills and your bank book. Examples include electricity, rates, road tax and TV licence.

As an alternative to using the Post Office facilities, you could consider a building society. In the past, people tended to think of building societies as places to save money, but now that attitude is changing as the range of services offered by building societies grows.

Different building societies offer different services so it pays to shop around, but all will write third-party cheques so that you can, for instance, collect a cheque made out to the electricity board and take it into the electricity board shop to pay your bill.

However, since this is a fairly cumbersome way of arranging your finances, a number of other schemes are in operation. The Halifax, the Abbey National and Town and Country societies, for example, issue cheque books so you can write cheques to pay bills but since they do not have cheque guarantee cards these cheque books will be of limited use – most shops would not accept cheques without a guarantee card.

Some building societies have links with credit card firms like Access. You use your card to make purchases and pay bills and when the Access bill comes in you simply take it along to the building society and they transfer money direct from your account to the credit card company. A handful of building societies even arrange for you to receive a credit card when you open an account with them.

Others may have cash dispensing cards on offer, so that you can get cash outside opening hours. And the Alliance Building Society runs something called the BankSave scheme in conjunction with the Bank of Scotland. At the beginning of each month, part of the money you pay into the building society is transferred into the bank. You have all the usual banking facilities – cheque book, overdrafts, loans and so on – but your bank account is only topped up by building society account when funds start to run low. This means that for at least part of each month your money earns interest in the building society.

Earning interest is one of the advantages of using the NSB or a building society. The other main one is that they are open outside normal daily banking hours and on Saturdays. But many women still find that the best way of handling their money is to have a bank account as well as a post office or building society account.

You could, of course, opt for an account with the National Girobank, which means you also have the advantage of the post office opening hours and the facility of cashing cheques and carrying out transactions at any post office. If you have an account with the National Girobank you get a chequebook, a cheque guarantee card and free banking so long as your account is in credit. (It is worth noting that most high street banks usually only offer free banking if you always keep a minimum of, say, £100, in your account.) If you do go into the red you get charged 30p for each transaction while you are overdrawn. (High street banks tend to charge you on *all* debits during a quarterly period if you drop below their limit at any time during that quarter.)

You can arrange standing orders and direct debits to pay regular bills through the National Girobank, just as you can with any of the high street banks. You can arrange personal loans, get travellers cheques and foreign currency, and have deposit or budget accounts. But you have no bank manager to talk to and you cannot arrange for an overdraft as you might be able to with a high street bank.

The National Girobank offers basic banking facilities, but the high street banks can offer much more. You have to decide whether you will need these. Do you need a credit card? Will you want to get money at odd times of the day or night from cash dispensing machines? Could a bank help you arrange a mortgage, help you with your tax, advise you on your investments, keep your valuables safe, or arrange insurance?

A market research report into banking services and the consumer, carried out in 1983, found that women were more likely than men to be ill at ease with their bank manager. But if you *do* have a high street bank account, then your bank manager can be an important ally in your struggle to keep financially afloat in these days of rising prices. To get him on your side, you have to treat him properly. Bank managers – like tax inspectors – do not really like being thought of as ogres. They want us all to know they are real human beings like the rest of us – and, given a chance, they will behave humanely. But what makes them hopping mad is customers who run up huge overdrafts without making prior arrangements.

You can probably get away with it once, or even twice. But if you are constantly deeply in the red then you will automatically be labelled as unreliable or a bad risk. Before this happens, you should summon up your courage and make an appointment to see your bank manager. If you are in financial difficulties he may be able to suggest a solution, but, in any case, the one thing a bank manager hates most of all is being kept in the dark. On the other hand, if you go asking for help, he may enjoy stepping in like Sir Galahad to the rescue.

Making an appointment to see the bank manager has a number of advantages. First, it is far more personal than writing letters and you may be able to impress him far more face to face than through a typewriter. Second, not only does it give him a chance to do his homework on you, but it gives you a chance to go armed with the kind of information he is bound to want.

If he is going to lend you money to tide you over – whether it is in the form of a loan or an overdraft – he will want to know where your money comes from and where it goes. Of course, he already knows quite a lot about your lifestyle – how many times a month you write cheques to the off-licence or the local boutiques, how much you earn – but it is always impressive to have a typed checklist of all your income, outgoings and capital. It makes it look as though you have *some* control over your money.

Bear in mind that overdrafts are cheaper than personal loans and always ask for more than you need. (Bank managers rarely lend the full amount requested.) Once you have been lent the cash, make sure you pay it back religiously within the agreed time. That way, you should have no problems borrowing again in the future.

And try to remember one key fact: banks would usually rather lend than not lend. *This is where they make their profits.*

Borrowing from the bank is only one kind of credit you may find useful. Others include Hire Purchase, Finance Company Loans, credit sale agreements and insurance policy loans. A leaflet, available from the Office of Fair Trading, called *There's More to Credit Than Just HP*, explains the advantages and disadvantages of each. (See also Chapter Six.)

Perhaps the kind of credit most of us use most often is the sort we get when we use credit cards, those ubiquitous oblongs of plastic. There are, of course, different types of credit cards: bank credit cards such as Access and Barclaycard; store credit cards; and charge cards like American Express and Diners Club.

## Bank credit cards

You can apply to any bank for its credit card, but usually you have to be a customer. Once you get the card you are given a credit limit and you can then use the card to get cash or pay for goods or meals, petrol or travel, or at any outlet which displays a sign showing it accepts the card. Every month you receive a statement showing how much you owe, including interest and any other charges.

The statement also tells you the minimum amount you have to pay off next month – you can pay more if you like, but not less. Credit cards can be handy – they mean you do not have to carry large sums of cash and they can help tide you over when funds are low if you think you will be more flush next month. But, and it is a big but, they can also be a great temptation. It is all too easy to get carried away with credit card spending because it does not somehow seem so real as paying cash or writing cheques and the total amount you owe may go on increasing as interest is added each month. In the end, the little number for sale at the local boutique that seemed such a bargain may cost you far more than you realized.

If you lose your credit card, let the comany know immediately so that the thief, or anyone finding the card, has no chance to go on a spending spree on your account.

One advantage to shopping by credit card is that you may get some extra consumer protection. Under the Consumer Credit Act, if you get faulty goods or services and you used a credit card to pay for them, you may be able to get satisfaction from the credit card company if you cannot settle matters with the retailer or the supplier. Your local Citizens' Advice Bureau, Consumer Advice Centre or Trading Standards Officer could advise you on this.

## Store credit cards and charge cards

Many large store groups operate their own credit card schemes. Some are the budget account type, where you are allowed to spend up to a certain limit – for example, twenty-four times the amount you can afford to pay each month. If this is £20, for instance, you limit will be £480. As you pay off your debt, you can top it up by making further purchases. But do not forget that interest will be added to your monthly statement, so just because you pay off £60 one month, does not mean you have £60 'in hand' to spend the next.

Another system used by some stores is to send you a bill at the end of each month for all items bought by credit card during that time. You then have to clear the debt altogether.

Store credit cards can be useful if you regularly buy a lot of items at that particular shop but, on the other hand, you are limited in your choice of goods to what the store sells.

The most famous charge cards are American Express and Diners Club. In theory, they do not actually give you credit – you are expected to pay your monthly statement in full when you get it. In practice, however, you get free credit from the time you use the card to pay for the goods or service until the time the statement arrives, itemizing those particular things. But you have to pay for this service through an initial enrolment fee and an annual charge for membership.

## Student grants

Having an American Express card or a wallet full of credit cards probably seems something of a joke if you are a student. Student grants do not go very far these days – that is if you can get one in the first place. The place to apply for a grant is your local education authority, that is the authority for the area where you will be resident or are normally resident on 30 June prior to the September when you are due to take up your place on a course.

If you are pursuing some form of advanced education on a 'designated course' such as a degree or an HND, qualify on the grounds of residency and have not undergone any kind of advanced education before, then you are entitled to a mandatory award. This will pay for your tuition fees and give you a grant over and above this which, in theory, is supposed to cover everything else – cost of accommodation, food, clothes, living expenses, travelling expenses.

The maximum grant you may be awarded varies according to whether you are living away from home or not, and whether or not 'away' means living in London. This next thing local education authorities take into account is whether you are 'independent' or not: to be classed in this category you must either be twenty-five *or* have supported yourself for three years. In either of these cases the authority will look at your income. In all other cases they look at that of your parents. And the grant you get will be reduced proportionately the more you or they earn. At present, for example, if you earn anything over £400 a year, your grant will go down accordingly. If your parents earn more than £7,600 the same applies. There is a cut-off point at about £17,000. From then on your parents could be multi-millionaires – you will still get the minimum £205. The maximum (if you are living away from home, but not in London) is £1,775 p.a.

If, however, you are not on a designated course for the first time you have to rely on the mercy of your local authority for a discretionary award. Most authorities do have some money available, but, as the National Union of Students point out, it is a small pot and there are always many applicants. There are no hard and fast rules governing who gets what. To a certain extent it is 'first come, first served', but it is also worth knowing that some courses appeal to local authorities more than others and so some applicants – such as medical students or lawyers – may have more of a chance than others. It is also worth realizing that authorities tend to favour those who have somehow missed out on higher education through no fault of their own rather than those who had a chance, dropped out and have had second thoughts. However, it is also worth bearing in mind that being turned down once may not be the end of the road. You can appeal against such a decision and appeals are sometimes successful.

The postgraduate situation is more complicated. Where you apply for funding depends to a large extent on the subject you will be studying. In general, though, post-graduate funding is hard to get, and you have to have a first class or a 2.1 honours degree to stand much of a chance.

If you have problems about grants then the first person to

contact is the welfare officer of your own student union. If the matter cannot be sorted out locally you will be referred to the National Union of Students. Sponsorships (where large firms or the Forces pay your way) exist, but are getting harder to come by. For a list of sponsoring bodies write to COIC, c/o Papworth Industries, Papworth Everard, Cambs CB3 8RG.

Many students take part-time or holiday jobs to make ends meet. It is worth knowing that your grant is tax free, so it cannot be added to any income for tax purposes. It is also worth knowing that if you are a single mother you are in a very strong position to claim Supplementary Benefit while you are studying full time since, being a single parent, you do not have to make yourself available for full-time work. Your local DHSS office are the people to contact if you think this could apply to you.

## State benefits

This brings us neatly to the subject of state benefits – except that the benefits system is anything but neat. Every time I read a story in the newspapers which says that, far from being a nation of scroungers, we do not claim thousands in benefits to which we are entitled, I feel not one iota of surprise. The DHSS publishes leaflets on most benefits but they often seem to require a degree in Advanced Jargon to follow. You can pick up these leaflets at your local DHSS office, but perhaps the best way to start is to get hold of a copy of a useful general booklet, also available there, called *Which Benefit? 60 ways you can get cash help*. This booklet (FB2), outlines the kinds of benefits for all situations and refers you to the specific leaflets in each case. You can also obtain it from the DHSS Leaflets Unit, PO Box 21, Stanmore, Middx.

To reduce the system to its simplest, there are two kinds of benefits available: contributory benefits (such as unemployment, sickness, and invalidity benefits) which you qualify for by contributing to the National Insurance scheme; and non-contributory benefits, which are not linked to the number of NI contributions you have made, but may be means-tested (such as supplementary benefit and family income supplement).

It can be very off-putting when you first visit a social security office to make a claim, since it always appears that everyone else but you knows the system. You may strike lucky and find a sympathetic and helpful clerk, but, there again, you might not. It is probably worth checking first with your local citizens' advice bureau to discuss with them all possibilities before you actually claim.

If you are a single parent, or divorced or separated, your financial situation will probably be far more complicated than if you are single in the strictest sense of the word. You may be entitled to additional benefits (see Chapter Eight) because you have children. You may be receiving maintenance, in which case the taxman may be involved. The tax system for maintenance is quite complicated and you can probably save money by discussing it fully with your own solicitor or your local tax office before finalizing arrangements.

Another good idea might be to seek advice from any of the organizations set up to help single parents, such as Gingerbread or the National Council for One Parent Families. Both produce a useful range of advice leaflets.

### Savings

Laughable though it may seem if you are struggling to make ends meet, it does pay to try to put some of your money away, if not regularly, then at least from to time. We all need some savings, whether they are for holidays, Christmas presents or those sudden emergencies when the washing machine floods the kitchen or the car breaks down.

Where you put your savings depends on a number of factors – how quickly you might need to lay your hands on the money, how much you can afford to put by regularly, and whether or not you are a taxpayer. Most people opt for building society or bank deposit accounts, Post Office savings accounts or government bonds. More speculative investments such as shares, unit trusts and unit-linked life insurance are really more suitable for long-term purposes rather than an emergency fund and, since all involve an element of gambling on what the economy will do over a number of years, are probably best avoided if making a loss would be disastrous. You could ask your bank manager for his advice or you could simply shop around until you find a savings scheme that suits your needs. Keep an eye on the financial pages of the newspapers – the *Daily Telegraph*, for instance, carries a feature called Savers Choice in its Saturday Family Money-Go-Round pages, which compares rates of interest in various saving schemes.

Knowing where your money goes is the first step towards knowing how much you can save. So fill in your cheque stubs. Keep bills and receipts – shove them all in a big box file, for example, and then every month have a glorious sort out. You do not have to be a financial genius to work out some kind of system. Just going through all your paperwork once a year will give you a pretty good idea of what lies ahead. Tot up how much you have spent in the past on regular commitments. Mark down on a wall chart or in your diary the dates when the big bills are likely to land with that sickening thud on your doormat – that way you will not be caught entirely unawares.

It is also worth investigating different ways of paying big bills since you do not *have* to wait for the quarterly account to come in. Take the electricity bill, for example. You could arrange for the board to estimate your total annual bills (based on previous years) and then pay a quarter of this amount four times a year, by direct debit or standing order through your bank. If, at the end of the year, it works out that you have been paying too much or too little, the figures are adjusted accordingly.

Another way of spreading the load throughout the year is by buying vouchers towards your quarterly bills as and when you can afford them. You can buy these at your high street showroom along with all the information about the different ways of paying.

You can also usually arrange to pay rates and water rates by monthly instalments and your local gas board probably runs a budget account scheme, where the total cost of your annual bills is estimated, spread over twelve months and adjusted at the end of the year.

To even out your big bills in this way can make life easier. But the main disadvantage is that there may be times during the year when you are actually in credit. In other words, you have money sitting in someone else's pocket, doing nothing for you.

The high street banks also run budget accounts to help you spread your bills over a year. These can take into account not only rates, gas and electricity, but phone bills, car tax and insurance, the cost of season tickets, insurance, holidays, clothing and so on. The Midland Bank, for instance, provides customers with a chart to estimate their year's bills and divide the total by twelve. This amount is then transferred monthly from the customer's current account into her Budget Account. The aim is that at the end of the year the monthly transfers and the bills will balance. Customers are given a Budget Account cheque book to pay for bills or they can arrange to do this through direct debits or standing orders.

However, banks do not run these schemes for nothing. You may have to pay interest and/or service charges. This is why the canny often organize their own budget accounts using building societies. You work out your annual outgoings in the same way and estimate how much money you need to set aside each month. But you pay this into a building society account and only withdraw the cash whenever you need it to pay a bill. The disadvantage is that you cannot go into the red, but the big advantage is that you are not charged for running the account *and* your money earns interest all the time it is there.

## Useful addresses and publications

Probably the best way to find out about the various services mentioned in this chapter is to walk into your local post office, banks or building societies and pick up the range of leaflets displayed there.

Among the publications on offer from the banks are:
'Our Survival Kit for Students' (Barclays)
'Personal Bank Charges and How to Avoid Them' (Barclays)
'When You Start Earning' (Lloyds)
'The NatWest Guide to Student Life' (National Westminster)

National Girobank information is available at post offices or from National Girobank, Bootle, Merseyside, G1R 0AA 051-966 2364.

The office of Fair Trading publishes a number of leaflets on credit including:
'There's More to Credit than Just HP'
'Equal Liability' (buying or selling on credit – who is responsible if things go wrong?)
These are available at Citizens' Advice Bureaux (check your phone book) or Trading Standards Departments (ditto).

The magazine *Which? Money* is published by the Consumers' Association and is available on subscription from them at 14, Buckingham Street, London WC2, 01-839 1222. Or you could check to see if your local library keeps copies.

*How to Manage Your Bank Manager* by John Duncan (a former NatWest manager) published by David and Charles, is also useful reading.

# 8

# The Single Woman and Children

There is an old joke about a woman who goes to see her doctor. After examining her the GP says: 'I have some good news for you Mrs Smith.' The woman interrupts: 'Actually, doctor, it's Miss Smith.' 'Ah,' says the doctor, 'in that case I have some bad news for you.'

These days single women can – and do – choose to have children and to bring them up alone. But for many single women pregnancy is not planned and can be an unwelcome event, at the very least, and total disaster at the very worst.

## Pregnancy testing

If you are single and think you may be pregnant the first thing to do is to make sure. The first sign is usually a missed period. Other symptoms can include tenderness in the breasts or nausea. Some women always know straight away if they are pregnant because they immediately go off alcohol or coffee. However, none of these things in themselves are absolute proof of pregnancy.

In the past, women often had to wait for a couple of months before they could be sure one way or another. These days you can find out if you are pregnant even before you have missed a period.

So what are the different pregnancy testing methods?

There are three types: a urine test on a slide, a urine test in a tube, and a blood test. All three work by detecting the presence of the hormone HCG, which is produced during pregnancy.

## Do-it-yourself pregnancy testing kits

Home pregnancy testing kits were first introduced in the 1970s and have proved to be about 98 per cent accurate if used correctly. The manufacturers now claim that they can be used even earlier than they used to be – anything from three to eight days after your period should have started. The kits can be bought from the chemist (prices range from £5.25 to £5.75) and all work in roughly the same way.

You get a test-tube containing some test reagent, a small tube of liquid and a test-tube holder with a mirror underneath it. You collect a small amount of early morning urine in a clean container, then add a few drops of this, plus a measured amount of the liquid provided, to the reagent in the test-tube. Shake the tube gently to mix everything up and then leave it, undisturbed, in the holder for either one or two hours, depending on which kit you use. After this time the result should be easy to read in the mirror.

Some of the kits contain two tests, so that you can double check a few days later if you initially had a negative result, but your period has still not started.

## GP and clinic tests

Most doctors will do a pregnancy test, free, for you. Some group practices carry out tests on the premises, but most GPs send off your early morning urine sample to the local hospital laboratories where it is tested on a slide. Most hospitals still use a test which accurately confirms pregnancy between twelve and fourteen days after the first day your period should have started. Recently, some have started to use a more sensitive test which can detect pregnancy just a few days after a missed period. In general, however, doctors prefer to wait for at least two weeks until they send off a sample to be tested, just in case your period is late for other reasons.

On top of this you may have to wait up to a week for the results to be sent back to your GP and if you want to know the good – or bad – news in a hurry it might be better to find an NHS family planning clinic or a private pregnancy advisory centre which could tell you the results the same day.

Family planning clinics will carry out a pregnancy test free; pregnancy advisory centres usually charge a fee of around £3 to £4. But both would probably advise you to wait until your period is between seven and fourteen days or more overdue.

You could also take a urine sample to a local chemist advertising pregnancy testing. The results should be available the same or the following day.

Finally, you could post a urine sample off to one of the British Pregnancy Advisory Service branches. Sent first class, it should arrive the following day and you could phone for the results. Their tests cost £3. (For phone numbers and addresses see the list at the end of this chapter.)

### Blood test (radioimmunoassay or RIA)

This test can confirm pregnancy ten days after conception – that is, before you even miss a period. You have to give a blood sample and because it uses radioactivity to show up the HCG, doctors need special equipment to carry it out. At present, therefore, this test is only available privately or through the Pregnancy Advisory Service in London for a fee of £6.

The kind of test you decide on depends on a number of factors – how soon you want to know whether you are pregnant or not, how much you can afford to pay, even where you live. Doing a test too soon may give a false negative result; using a urine sample that is contaminated or too dilute can also affect the test. And it is easy to get false result on a home testing kit if you do not follow the instructions carefully.

Once you have confirmed your pregnancy, you should see a doctor as soon as possible – and that holds good whether you want to have the baby or not. Studies have shown that it is best for both babies and mother if ante-natal care begins as soon as possible. And very early abortion is both safer and generally less traumatic.

### Abortion

Despite the anti-abortionists who suggest that these days abortion is virtually available on demand, the fact is that you cannot have an abortion just because you want one. Under the 1967 Abortion Act you need the consent of two doctors who have to sign a form saying they genuinely believe that either there is a real risk of the baby being born handicapped, or that continuing the pregnancy would affect your physical or mental health or the would affect your physical or mental health or the physical or mental health of any existing children, or that your life would be at risk if you continued with the pregnancy. (In Scotland the law is slightly different but, in practice, works the same way as in England and Wales. In Northern Ireland it is much more strict which is why many women come to England from Northern Ireland to have an abortion.)

Arranging an abortion is not always easy and it varies greatly, depending on where you live. It *is* possible to get an abortion on the National Health Service, but about half the abortions carried out in Great Britain are performed by private agencies, partly because they can often offer a quicker service than the NHS and partly because some women may find their own GP less than co-operative.

Unless you really do not want to see your own GP, you should visit him as soon as you think you are pregnant. Explain why you do not want to have the baby and if he refuses to help, ask why. It may be that he genuinely feels you do not qualify for an abortion under the Act – or he may be following his religious views or his conscience. If he does not want to help on moral grounds, ask him to refer you to a colleague.

If you have made up your mind that you want an abortion, do not let your GP bamboozle you with delaying tactics – like suggesting you come back after a few weeks to see if you have missed another period. Ask for an immediate referral or go elsewhere for help.

Assuming that your GP is helpful, the next step will be for him to refer you to a hospital doctor, who has to agree that you qualify for an abortion and that he or his staff will do it. Once again, this is where time can be wasted. It may take time for you to have your initial interview, it may take more time to be booked in for the operation. You may even find that the consultant has less liberal views than your GP – and after all the delays you will be back to square one.

If you cannot get an NHS abortion, or if you would rather pay and avoid all the delays and complications this may involve, it is probably best to turn to one of the non-profit making registered charities who carry out abortions.

The British Pregnancy Advisory Service has around thirty full or part-time branches throughout Britain and five nursing homes which carry out abortions, at Bournemouth, Brighton, Doncaster, Leamington Spa and Liverpool (see list of addresses at the end of this chapter).

The Pregnancy Advisory Service and the Marie Stopes House, whose offices are both in central London, also have their own nursing home, and although these two organizations are London based, they do see women from all over the country.

You do not have to be referred to any of these clinics by your GP, although PAS say that about half their clients are; you can simply phone and make an appointment.

It is no good thinking you can just pop in during your lunch hour for this initial consultation because it can be quite a lengthy process. The DHSS lays down fairly strict regulations which have to be followed carefully.

To begin with, you will be seen by a counsellor who will talk you through your problems and the reasons why you are considering an abortion. This gives you a chance to examine your feelings and an opportunity to change your mind. Diane Munday of BPAS says that between 10 and 12 per cent of women who attend their clinics decide not to have abortions after all.

After this you will be seen by a doctor. At the PAS one doctor talks to you about your contraceptive problems, then another gives you a thorough medical examination to confirm your pregnancy, check your general health and gynaecological history, and see whether or not you are fit enough for an operation. Finally, you will be booked in for the termination of the pregnancy at the nursing home.

Costs vary slightly. BPAS charge £22 for the initial consultation, PAS £20. Marie Stopes charge £133 for an abortion carried out up to thirteen weeks of pregnancy, £160 up to eighteen weeks. PAS charge £120 up to fourteen weeks, £145 up to nineteen weeks, and £210 up to twenty-two weeks. BPAS charges go from £105 for early abortions, £210 for later ones and £252 for ones over twenty weeks.

There are also some commercial abortion agencies who, like the charities, are controlled by the DHSS. Many offer a perfectly good service, but prices are usually higher than those charged by the non-profit making agencies.

If money is a problem, the charities will do what they can to help. Most of them offer some kind of easy payment scheme so you do not have to find all the cash before you have the abortion. So, however poor or desperate you are, DO NOT try do-it-yourself methods. Most of the old folk remedies either do not work or could kill you. At the very least you could impair your fertility for ever or end up still pregnant and giving birth to a handicapped baby.

The kind of abortion available usually depends on how far advanced pregnancy is. Up to twelve weeks the most common way is by vacuum aspiration. (It is worth knowing that doctors date pregnancy not by the day you conceived but by the first day of your last period. So by the time your period is one day late you will already be four weeks pregnant, not two.)

Vacuum aspiration can be done under a general or a local anaesthetic and you may be able to go home the same day or you may be kept in overnight for observation.

A small tube is passed through your vagina and into your womb via the neck of the cervix. If you are only a few weeks pregnant it may not be necessary to widen the cervix to get the tube in: in later weeks it may have to be stretched slightly to allow a larger tube to be used. Once the tube is in place, the contents of the womb are removed using a suction pump.

Later abortions can be carried out by dilation and curettage (a 'D and C'). This is a procedure done under a general anaesthetic and involves dilating or stretching the cervix so that the contents of the womb can be scraped out.

A third method, used for late abortions, is more like inducing labour. Substances, such as prostaglandins or saline, are injected into the womb, causing it to contract and expel the foetus. This usually happens within twelve to thirty-six hours but may, in any case, have to be followed by a D and C to make sure none of the placenta has been left behind. It can be very distressing to go through this kind of fake labour – and that is just one reason why it is best, if abortion is what you want, to organize it as soon as possible.

Another, probably more compelling, factor is that of safety. One American study has shown that the risk of dying if you have abortion at under eight weeks pregnancy is 1 for every 100,000 abortions. This goes up to 24 for every 100,000 abortions at sixteen to twenty weeks and to more than 34 at twenty-one weeks or more.

Of course, any operation which requires a general anaesthetic involves some risk. But are there other risks in abortion? Many doctors feel it can be proved that it is actually safer to have an early abortion than it is to go on and have a baby, since motherhood still carries some risk to life and health, even today. But abortions can lead to infection or excessive bleeding and, if you have a D and C, there may be a slightly higher chance of premature labour, low birth-weight and even miscarriage in the fourth to sixth months of a following pregnancy, possibly because of slight damage to the cervix, although the latest studies seem to disprove this.

Most women feel completely fit and well within a couple of days of an abortion. You can expect vaginal bleeding for a few days and you may have mild period pains. It is best to take things easy for a week or two and if you have excess discharge, any sudden or heavy bleeding, and severe or persistent pain, or a high temperature, then you should see a doctor at once.

## Adoption

Abortion is, of course, just one of the options open to the single woman who faces an unplanned pregnancy. Continuing with the pregnancy and having the baby adopted, though rarer than it used to be, is still a course of action some women choose.

If you think you want your baby to be adopted, the first step might be to ask to see the hospital social worker at the ante-natal clinic where your pregnancy is being monitored. She will be able to give you advice and to put you in touch with your local social services department, who may arrange adoptions. Or you could contact the social services department yourself. Another alternative, if you have strong views on what kind of adoptive parents you would like for your baby, might be to go direct to an adoption agency – if you wanted the child brought up as a Catholic, for instance, you might approach the Catholic Children's Society. A full list of adoption agencies can be obtained from the British Agencies for Adoption and Fostering.

When you go into hospital to have the baby, be prepared to cope with the attitudes of some of the nurses and midwives who might not understand why you want your child adopted. Hospital policy after the baby is born varies – some will happily keep the baby for seven days, even if you are discharged after two. Usually, a baby is placed in a foster home for the first six weeks, while you are given time to think things over. During this time a social worker or counsellor will talk the matter through with you and explain the adoption procedure. You will also be given a written explanation.

After six weeks the baby is usually given to the prospective adoptive parents, but they cannot apply to the courts to adopt your child until it has lived with them for three months. You will be asked to give your consent in writing before the adoption order can be made. But you can withdraw your consent any time you want to, right up to the final day of the court hearing *unless* you have previously agreed to the 'freeing' procedure. Under this you sign a form which effectively declares you have no further interest in the child and gives the adoption agency the right to choose adoptive parents as well as parental responsibility and rights over the child until the adoption is completed.

Once a child has been 'freed' like this, you cannot stop an adoption going through unless your child is still waiting for a new family a year after the freeing order was made. The adoption laws are very complicated and, even if you change your mind about having your baby adopted, there are certain circumstances in which the courts could order an adoption without your consent.

But if the court is considering doing this, it must tell you why and give you a chance to get a solicitor and apply for legal aid.

Incidentally, beware of anyone who suggests arranging a private, no-fuss adoption. You could run into trouble with the law. The only people allowed to adopt without using an adoption agency are close relatives, such as your parents, or your brothers or sisters.

## Getting help

A third course of action you may choose is to have the baby and bring it up yourself. But whether you decide to do this or whether you decide to have the baby adopted, you may need help during your pregnancy. Apart from any support and information you may be able to get from your social services department concerning grants, allowances and so on, there are a number of charities you could also turn to.

LIFE can offer telephone help and advice and non-abortion counselling. Local groups can provide moral support and practical aid – maybe to provide emergency accommodation, see you through the form-filling needed to get social security and maternity benefits, take you to ante-natal clinics or help find furniture for a flat or baby clothes. The charity also runs LIFE houses to provide accommodation for single homeless girls during their pregnancy and for up to six months afterwards.

Another useful organization to contact is the National Council for One Parent Families. Like LIFE, they offer a free and confidential counselling service which can offer help and advice on legal matters, housing problems, social security and so on. They also publish a number of leaflets which may be helpful, including *Single and Pregnant*, a guide to benefits for single pregnant women and pregnant mothers.

The Health Education Council has produced a useful book called, simply, *Pregnancy Book* which, amongst other invaluable information, clearly sets out the rights and benefits available. These are some of the main ones:

## Maternity grant

*What?* This is a lump sum, paid by girocheque (currently £25).

*Who?* All pregnant women who have lived in this country for at least six of the twelve months before their baby is due can get the maternity grant; if you claim after the baby's birth, you must have lived in this country for at least six of the twelve months before the birth.

*When?* You can claim at any time from the twenty-sixth week of your pregnancy up to three months after your baby is born. But if you are applying for maternity allowance too, (it is on the same form) it is important to make an early claim.

*How?* Get form BM4 from your ante-natal clinic, your GP, your midwife, your health visitor or your social security office. You will also need a certificate of expected confinement, saying when your baby is due. Your doctor or midwife can give you this. If you claim after your baby is born his birth certificate will do instead. Send the certificate with the form to your local social security office.

## Maternity allowance

*What?* This is a weekly payment. It is usually paid for eighteen weeks, starting eleven weeks before your baby is due. If your baby is late, the allowance will be paid for longer – until six weeks after the baby is born. It is paid by a book of orders which you cash at the post office each week. The allowance will not be paid for any days that you are working. (It is currently £25.45 per week plus 15p per dependent child.)

*Who?* Whether you qualify depends on your previous National Insurance contributions. The rules are explained in the leaflet N117A which you can obtain from your social security office or ante-natal clinic. Claim:

—if you have worked at all during the last two years or so,
—if you were at school, a student or an apprentice during the past two years,

—even if you have not paid the full NI contributions to get the full allowance; you may still get part of it.

Send the claim to your local social security office and they will work out if you are eligible.

*When?* Claim as soon as possible after the twenty-sixth week of pregnancy, even if you are still working and even if you do not have your certificate of expected confinement. You can send this later.

*How?* Claim on form BM4 (see above).

## Free prescriptions and NHS dental treatment

*Who?* All pregnant women and mothers for one year after the baby is born.

*How?* For free prescriptions, get form FW8 from your doctor, midwife or health visitor. Send the completed form to your Family Practitioner Committee (address in local phone book).Or, after the baby is born, get form P11 from your post office or social security office. For free dental treatment, simply tell your dentist when you go.

## Free milk and vitamins

*Who?* All pregnant women and families with a child under five who are on supplementary benefit or family income supplement or whose income is low.

*How?* If you are on supplementary benefit or family income supplement, claim on part of Form FW8 available from your doctor, midwife or health visitor. If you are not on SB or FIS, but your income is low, get leaflet MV11 from your post office, social security office or chemist.

## Supplementary benefit

*What?* This is a weekly allowance. It is paid by a book of orders you cash at the post office or by Girocheque.

*Who?*  You can claim if you are not in full-time work and your income is below a certain level. You cannot claim if you are under sixteen.

*How?*  If you are unemployed, get form B1 from the unemployment office. Otherwise, get form SB1 from your social security office or post office. Send your form to your social security office. You will be given an appointment for an interview. If you need money urgently, phone or call at the social security office and explain.

*When?*  If you have to claim supplementary benefit when you give up work to have a baby, claim:

—within the first week after you stop work, if you are paid weekly,

or

—towards the end of the first month after you stop work, if you are paid monthly.

You do not have to register as unemployed if you stopped work when you were twenty-nine weeks pregnant, nor if you stopped earlier, so long as your doctor has signed a certificate to say you were not well enough to work. Nor do you have to register as unemployed if you are a single parent with children under sixteen.

Remember to tell the social security office when your baby is born so that you get the extra allowance for a dependent child.

## If you get supplementary benefit you can also get:

—Help towards housing costs
—Extra help towards heating costs if you have special needs
—Free NHS dental treatment
—Free NHS glasses
—Free prescriptions
—Free milk and vitamins for pregnant women and children under five

—Free school meals

—Fares for hospital appointments refunded.

## You may also be able to get single payments

*What?* These are lump sums paid to help with special expenses like things for the baby and maternity clothes for you.

*Who?* You can claim if you are entitled to supplementary benefit and have only a certain amount of savings.

*How?* Ask your social security office how to claim.

*When?* You can claim from the thirty-fourth week of your pregnancy and for up to a year after your baby is born.

## Child benefit

*What?* This is a cash benefit for each child under sixteen (or under nineteen if still at school). It is normally paid every four weeks through a book of orders which you cash at the post office.

*Who?* All mothers who have been living in Great Britain for at least six months can claim child benefit. You can get it whatever your income.

*How?* Get forms CH2 and CH3 and leaflet CH1 from your social security office (if they were not sent to you when you claimed your maternity grant). Fill them in and return them. If you are claiming for a new baby for the first time, you have to send the baby's birth certificate.

*When?* Claim as soon as possible after you have registered your baby's birth. If you are not getting benefit for a child or children you already have, claim at once.

## One parent benefit

*What?* This is an extra payment to those bringing up a child on their own. It is usually paid with your child benefit in one order book.

*Who?* You can claim if you are single, divorced or permanently separated. You cannot claim if you are living with someone as a couple.

*How?* Claim on form CH11.

*When?* If you are separated, claim when the separation is made legal or when you are divorced, or when you have been living apart for thirteen weeks, whichever comes first. Otherwise, claim at once.

## Family income supplement

*What?* This is a benefit for working families on low pay. The amount you get depends on what you earn and how many children you have. It is paid by a book of orders which normally lasts for a year whether or not your wages go up or the size of your family changes. You can claim it as well as child benefit or single parent benefit.

*Who?* A single parent can claim if she works twenty-four hours a week or more.

*How?* Claim on form FIS 1 from your post office or social security office. Send the completed form to the address on the form, not to your social security office. You will also need to send five payslips if you are paid weekly, or two if you are paid monthly.

*When?* Claim as soon as possible after your baby is born. If you get FIS you can also get free school meals, NHS dental treatment, NHS glasses, free milk and vitamins for pregnant women and children under five, and fares for hospital appointments refunded.

## Tax allowances

Single mothers can claim an additional personal allowance to bring their tax allowance up to the married man's level. Once your baby is born, contact your local tax office.

For rights concerning maternity pay, leave and the right to return to work, see Chapter Two.

## Becoming a single mother

Not all single mothers become so by accident. A small, but significant, number of single women decide each year that they want a child of their own, but not necessarily a man as well. Some are involved in lesbian relationships. Others simply want to experience motherhood rather than marriage. Others just have not met Mr Right, but feel that they want a baby before it is 'too late'.

Adopting a baby is almost certainly out: to start with, there just are not enough babies to go round and most adoption agencies will not consider single people as adoptive parents for babies, although they might for children with special needs. Alternatively, it might be possible for a single woman to be accepted as a foster parent. You should remember, however, that the agencies are not there to fulfil your frustrated maternal longings, but to serve best the needs of the children they represent.

However, if you are interested in finding out more about adoption or fostering, the British Agencies for Adoption and Fostering publish a number of useful booklets.

In most cases, though, if you want a baby you will have to have one of your own – and that means finding a man to help you conceive or paying to be artificially inseminated by the sperm of a donor.

Whichever method you choose, you need to know when you are ovulating. One way is to take your temperature each morning when you wake and keep a record of it. A woman who is ovulating normally will see that around the middle of her cycle her temperature dips slightly, then rises, and stays at the higher level until her period starts. It is when the dip shows that ovulation occurs. You can buy a clinical thermometer at the chemist's and it usually comes with a special graph or grid ready for you to complete day by day. If you are ill, have drunk lots of alcohol or done anything out of the ordinary, you should mark this on the chart against the appropriate day as this can affect the temperatures. You really need to keep a record for several months so that you become used to the way your cycles usually go.

Another do-it-yourself method of checking ovulation is to

examine your vaginal secretions every day. The cells of the cervix secrete mucus during the entire cycle, but this changes throughout the month.

Each time mucus production begins in a cycle it is usually thick, opaque, white or yellowy, scant and sticky. As ovulation approaches, the mucus becomes cloudy and then clear, more fluid, transparent and elastic. Just before ovulation it is thin, slippery and stretchy. After ovulation it changes again – there may be virtually none at all or it may become sticky and cloudy again. For the first few months of using this method it may be helpful to keep a record of your observations. Many women combine this way of checking ovulation with a temperature chart.

An egg lives about a day and sperms for about two or three days, so you need to bear this in mind as well. Other tips, if you are trying to get pregnant, whichever method you are using, include:

—having an orgasm after sperm is inside you (this helps the uterus suck up sperms more actively),
—remain lying down for at least half an hour with a pillow under your hips so the semen can form a pool around the cervix,
—do not wash or douche your vagina immediately before or afterwards,
—if you need lubrication use saliva, not creams or jellies.

Ironic although it may seem to anyone who has spent years trying *not* to get pregnant, the reverse may prove just as complicated. Western women are at their most fertile around the age of twenty-five but after that fertility begins to decrease. After the age of thirty it declines fairly rapidly. And, in any case, even couples who make love on an unrestricted basis take an average time of 5.3 months to conceive.

So, if you have a male volunteer lined up to act as a kind of stud, or if you are planning to seduce some unsuspecting man and simply keep the fact that you are hoping to get pregnant a secret, you have to bear in mind that you may be committed to more than a one-night stand.

Of course, you do not have to make love to a man to get pregnant. AID (artificial insemination by donor) is a technique developed to help couples where the man has fertility problems, but it can also be used by single women who want a child.

Donor semen, either fresh or previously deep-frozen and stored in a sperm bank, is introduced into a woman's vagina either by a plastic syringe or a special cap which is held against the cervix. The woman remains lying down for about half an hour and is told not to wash or douche for at least twelve hours after the treatment.

Finding an AID clinic which is prepared to consider a single woman for treatment, however, requires the sleuthing abilities of Sherlock Holmes plus loads of determination. It is simply a question of finding as many clinics as you can and asking each in turn.

Some of the charities which offer contraceptive and abortion advice also offer AID; your local family planning clinic or citizens' advice bureau may have lists of centres offering AID locally: if your NHS hospital runs an AID clinic you may be able to find out if the consultants there also have private practices. As a last resort you could contact the National Association for the Childless (see the list of addresses at the end of this chapter) since they have a list of some of the clinics in Britain.

Costs vary. A typical charge at a private clinic could be £40 a session.

Of course, if you know a man who is prepared to act as a donor you do not need to go to a clinic. All you need is a supply of fresh sperm, a container to collect it in (say a glass or an egg cup) and something to get the sperm from the container into the vagina (a syringe or even one of the applicators sold with tubes of spermicide). If you want to know more about self-insemination, the Feminist Self Insemination Group have published a pamphlet which is available from Sisterwrite, 190 Upper Street, London N1, or you can write to the group c/o the bookshop.

Before any single woman decides to have a child on her own, whether she becomes pregnant by accident or design, she should think very carefully about the consequences.

One of the advantages of being a single unmarried mother is that you are the legal guardian of your children and you automatically have custody with all the rights that entails –

deciding how to bring them up and what kind of schools they go to. You decide what name to register them under and, even if the child's father suddenly discovers all kinds of paternal longings, you can prevent him from seeing the child unless he has a court order allowing access.

The disadvantages can be both emotional and practical. Unless you are very rich, being a single mother can be a tremendous financial strain. Babies cost more than you think. Growing children cost even more. And even if you have a reasonably paid job to return to, finding the right kind of childcare within your means can be very difficult (see Chapter Two).

On top of this is the 24-hour responsibility of caring for a tiny, dependent creature. It can be hard enough coping when there is someone else to share the disturbed nights, the mound of washing, the sheer strain of worrying about whether a child is eating enough, sleeping enough and why it is crying. A real baby is very different from the cuddly bundles you see in advertisements. More to the point, it grows into a tantrum-throwing toddler, an awkward schoolchild, a difficult adolescent. You are not just having a baby – you are committing yourself to at least eighteen years of motherhood. And if you cannot cope, if the local council feel you are incapable of looking after your child properly, you could find it being taken into care.

However, there are lots of places you can turn to for help long before you get to this sorry state. You may find it useful to discuss problems with your GP, your midwife or your health visitor. You can also build up friendships with other mothers you will meet at your child health clinic. More specifically, the National Childbirth Trust not only runs ante-natal classes, but can also offer practical advice and support after the baby is born. The NSPCC also gives practical help to people having difficulties with their children.

MAMA (Meet-a-Mum Association) holds social gatherings and offers support on a mother-to-mother basis using volunteers who have themslves coped with post-natal problems such as depression or isolation. And Parents Anonymous runs a 24-hour telephone answering service for parents who feel they cannot cope or might abuse their children. (Addresses and telephone numbers are at the end of this chapter.)

Not all single mothers are single in the sense of being unmarried or alone. Some may be living with a man in a relationship which is, in many ways, like marriage. Others may be second-time around singles – the separated, the divorced or the widowed.

There are two books which provide useful information for the single mother who is living with someone: *Living Together* by Clare Dyer and Marcel Berlins and *The Cohabitation Guide* by Pat Clayton.

And second-time around singles may find it useful to read *Going Solo* by Jacqueline Dineen and *Divorce and Your Children* by Anne Hooper.

Second-time around single mothers not only have to cope with all the problems any single mother faces, they also have to see their children through the kind of practical and emotional upheaval that divorce or widowhood can cause. When a marriage breaks up it is all too easy for children to become pawns in some kind of battle between warring parents. Access to fathers, for instance, is often denied or given grudgingly.

Yet all the evidence shows that children adjust best to divorce if they maintain good relationships with both parents, however hard this might be to arrange. Sometimes it can help to bring in a third party as a kind of referee before things get too bad. Marriage guidance counsellors can provide this kind of divorce counselling or conciliation. You can find your local marriage guidance service by checking in the phone directory or by contacting the National Marriage Guidance Council in Rugby.

Another source of help and support for the single mother, whatever her circumstances, is Gingerbread, an association for one-parent families. Gingerbread runs a network of local self-help groups and provides both social contact with other adults as well as practical and moral support on a wide range of problems. Gingerbread groups have organized babysitting pools to allow lone parents a night out, clothes and toy pools, skill exchanges, a listening-ear service for desperate parents and support by accompanying each other to see solicitors, attend court hearings, go to the social services and so on.

To help those who have to work, some Gingerbread groups have organized their own day-care schemes and some groups have also set up their own Advice Offices, staffed either by volunteers or by professional staff to give welfare rights advice to one-parent families. Gingerbread also publishes a number of Welfare Leaflets covering all kinds of aspects from 'Day Care' to 'Access – how to make it easier for your children'.

## Sterilization

The bulk of this chapter has concentrated on the single woman and children on the way or already here. But what of the future? If a single woman decides she never wants children or that she wants to have no more, can she take the final step and have a sterilization?

In theory, the answer is yes. In practice it may be more difficult. Doctors know only too well that even married couples who appear to have thought things through carefully may return a few years after a sterilization asking about the possibilities of a reversal. This makes them extremely reluctant to agree to sterilize a single woman.

However, your chances are better if you already have children and if you are older rather than younger. This said, if you are persistent enough, you can probably find a doctor who would agree to carry out the operation for you. You would also have to be able to pay, since there is a long queue for NHS sterilizations and you would hardly be seen as a priority, if you were accepted on the NHS at all.

There are various techniques used for female sterilization, but they all involve cutting or tying the Fallopian tubes so that egg and sperm never meet. The operation usually involves an overnight or a few days' stay in hospital. You can ask your doctor to refer you to a hospital consultant if you want to try the NHS. Private operations, including day-care treatment, are available from Marie Stopes House, British Pregnancy Advisory Service or by referral to a consultant from a GP.

The approximate cost varies from around £100 to £200

(depending on technique, length of stay etc.) and in *all* cases you should get counselling advice before the operation.

Sterilization is not a step to be taken lightly. The prospect of motherhood may appal you when you are in your twenties, for instance, but by the time you are thirty-five you may be positively broody. Although reversals are sometimes possible, you cannot bank on it. If you are sterilized you have to accept that you have said 'no' to babies for ever.

## Useful addresses

British Pregnancy Advisory Service (Head Office) Austy Manor, Wootton Wawen, Solihull, West Midlands, B95 6BX, Henley in Arden 3225.

*Branches* (The range of services varies from branch to branch):
Basingstoke: 0256 59720 (24-hour answering service),
                   0256 53129 Wednesdays and Fridays 6-8 p.m.
Bath: 02217 3321 (24-hour answering service)
Bedford: 0234 46574 (24-hour answering service)
Birmingham: 021-643 1461 (24-hour answering service)
Bournemouth: 0202 28762 (24-hour answering service)
Bradford: 0274 44483 Tuesdays 5 p.m. to 10 p.m.
Brighton: 0273 509726 (24-hour answering service)
Cardiff: 0222 372389 (24-hour answering service)
Chester: 0244 27113 (24-hour answering service)
Coventry: 0203 597344 (24-hour answering service)
Doncaster: 0302 4893 (24-hour answering service)
Glasgow: 041 204 1832 (24-hour answering service)
Hull: 0482 223944 (24-hour answering service)
Leamington Spa: 0203 597344 (24-hour answering service)
Leeds: 0532 443861 (24-hour answering service)
Liverpool: 051-227 3721 (24-hour answering service)
London: 01-222 0985 (24-hour answering service)
Luton: 0582 26287 (24-hour answering service)
Manchester: 061-236 7777 (24-hour answering service)
Milton Keynes: 0908 663601 (24-hour answering service)
Peterborough: 0733 270763 Monday to Friday 6-7.15 p.m.

Sheffield: 0742 738326 (24-hour answering service)
Southampton: 0703 334196 (24-hour answering service)
Swindon: 0793 30366 (24-hour answering service)
    0793 813450 Thursdays 6 p.m. to 8 p.m.
Telford: 0952 598 323 Monday to Friday 9 a.m. to 6 p.m.

Pregnancy Advisory Service:   11-13 Charlotte Street, London W1, 01-637 8962

Marie Stopes House:   Well Woman Centre, 108 Whitfield Street, London W1, 01-388 0662.

British Agencies for Adoption and Fostering:   11 Southwark St, London SE1 1RQ, 01-407 8800.

LIFE:   7 Parade, Leamington Spa, Warwick. 0926 21587.

National Council for One Parent Families:   255 Kentish Town Road, London NW5 2LX, 01-267 1361.

Health Education Council:   78 New Oxford Street, London WC1A 1AH, 01-637 1881

National Association for the Childless:   318, Summer Lane, Birmingham B19 3RL, 021-359 4887.

National Childbirth Trust:   9 Queensborough Terrace, London W2 3TB, 01-221 3833.

NSPCC:   67 Saffron Hill, London EC1N 8RF, 01-242 1626.

MAMA:   to contact a local group please write, with a sae to 26A Cumnor Hill, Oxford OX3 9HA.

Parents Anonymous:   6 Manor Gardens, London N7 6LA, 01-263 8918 (24-hour answering service).

OPUS:   Organisation for Parents Under Stress, Great Carr Farm, Kirby Misperton, Malton, N. Yorks. 0653 86256.

National Marriage Guidance Council: Herbert Gray College, Little Church Street, Rugby CV21 3AP, 0788 73241.

Gingerbread:   To contact a local group write or phone head office: 35 Wellington St, London WC2, 01-240 0953.

*Advice centres*

Barking and Dagenham: 01-517 0008
Birmingham: 021-622 5905
Bradford: 0274 307665
Bristol: 0272 291705
Cambridge: 0223 321562
Dartford: 0322 28769
Hull: 0482 23355
Keighley: 0535 69752
Leeds: 0532 459580 (Thursday 10 a.m. to 12 noon)
Liverpool: 051-708 8848
Manchester: 061-248 6739
Mansfield: 0623 642509
Newcastle: 0632 328751
Peacehaven: 07914 87159
Plymouth: 0752 21048
Redcar: 0642 479911
Scunthorpe: 0724 872862
Stoke on Trent: 0782 82178
Stoke on Trent: 0782 821401
Swindon: 0793 26415

*Wales*

Cardiff: 0222 384877 (Mondays/Wednesdays/Fridays 11
a.m.-3 p.m.)

*Scotland*

Aberdeen: 0224 22854 (Thursdays 2 p.m.-8 p.m.)
Dundee: 0382 29378
Edinburgh: 031-229 0923 (Mondays/Wednesdays/Fridays
10 a.m.-2.30 p.m.)
Glasgow: 041-248 6840
Livingston: 0506 35985

*Ireland*

Belfast: 692960
Dublin: 710291

## Useful publications

Anna Coote and Tess Gill, *Women's Rights, A Practical Guide*, Penguin. Has chapters on divorce and on children.

Clare Dyer and Marcel Berlins, *Living Together*, Hamlyn.

Pat Clayton, *The Cohabitation Guide*, Wildwood House.

Jacqueline Dineen, *Going Solo*, Unwin paperbacks.

Patricia Ashdown Sharp, *A Single Woman's Guide to Pregnancy and Parenthood*, Penguin.

# 9
# The Single Woman on Holiday

It happens every year before the Christmas tree has finished shedding all its needles or the last of the mince pies has gone stale. You only have to turn on the television or pick up a newspaper or magazine to be wooed with promises of idyllic fortnights spent on sun-soaked islands or get-away-from-it-all cruises down the Nile. The holiday booking season has come round again.

But if you are a single woman what are the holiday prospects like? Should you try to find someone else to go with or should you take the plunge and spend your hard-earned cash on a solo holiday? And what kind of holiday would be best?

Picking a holiday partner can be tricky. The idea of spending two weeks away with the latest man in your life may seem heavenly in January. But by June what do you do if the relationship is already beginning to lose its lustre? Cancelling the trip altogether will cost you money. Going ahead could be purgatory. Even long-established couples can find the 24-hour togetherness of holidays hard to take – something which often comes as a shock since we all like to think of holidays as magical, perfect times.

Going away with a special girl friend can also be fraught with dangers. Maybe your idea of a holiday is to spend as long as possible soaking up the sun; she gets sunburnt even when she plasters herself head to toe in Factor 7 sun lotion. Or you like visiting churches and museums to find out about local customs and history while her idea of getting to know a country is to sit in a bar and work her way through the local cocktails.

Going with a group of friends – renting a villa together, for instance – can be one answer. But not all single women have enough friends who can all arrange to take holidays at the same time, or who could agree on where to go or what kind of holiday to take.

Luckily, whether you decide to plan a solo holiday through choice or necessity, the options for a single woman have never been greater. Ordinary package deal holidays are probably best avoided. During the days you will probably be able to keep busy doing whatever you like best, whether it is reading the latest bestseller as you soak up the sun by the pool or joining the excursions to the local wine factory or underground caves. But in the evenings you will probably feel the odd girl out as the dining room and bar fills up with families and couples. After a few evenings you will either be going potty for someone to talk to or you will be fending off the unwelcome attentions of every Tomas, Enrico or Ari of the hotel staff who think you must be fair game.

A better idea might be to join a *villa party*. There are now quite a lot of holiday firms who specialize in arranging these. Small World, for example, run villa parties in countries like Turkey, Menorca and Greece and they also have winter chalet parties in places like Switzerland, France and Italy. You share a villa with others – some single, some couples – in groups ranging from about ten to twenty five. The company employs girls to do the cooking (and sometimes the cleaning, too) and to arrange events like barbecues or midnight ski-ing. The idea is that you can spend as much or as little time as you wish together as a group, but that you do have the chance to meet up over an evening meal and talk about the day's events. Of course, you have to take pot luck on what the other members of the group will be like, but if it is large enough the chances are that at least one other person will be sympatico.

Small World say that about 30 per cent of their bookings are from people holidaying alone and they do split their villa parties into two age groups – the 20s to 30s and the 30s to 40s.

## Package holidays

Another area you could consider are the *young, fun holiday packages*.

There has been quite a boom in recent years in the number of companies offering package deals aimed at the under-30s. Not all of these put a specific age limit on their potential customers but, as one of the brochures puts it: 'For sure we are not about family holidays. There are no kids or grannies'.

Young World is just one of the companies which runs holidays for the 18 to 30s. You can stay in a thatched hut at Camp Africa in Morocco, in Greek villas on the island of Thassos, in tents at Suncamp France near Perpignan or in a hotel room or an apartment at Es Canar in Ibiza. Young World also run winter sports holidays in Soldeu, Andorra and Livigno, Italy.

Your travel agent will be able to give you details of other companies which cater specifically for the 18 to 35 age range, whose customers book in pairs, in groups or solo. The choice of resorts should range from places such as Majorca to Ibiza to Corfu and Kos.

Most of the companies try to disassociate themselves with the popular image of the young 'fun' holidaymaker whose idea is to get smashed each night and indulge in what might politely be called bed-hopping and/or high spirits. Yet it must be said that some of the 'young, fun holidays' can turn out to be nothing less than disasters unless it is your idea of fun to indulge in the kind of over-the-top behaviour that gives English girls a bad name abroad.

Another alternative is the holiday specially designed for *singles*. If you belong to any of the contact clubs mentioned in Chapter Four, you may find they organize their own holidays. Or you may like to look at the brochures of companies like Blue Sky and Enterprise which offer singles holidays.

Before you book any holiday it is worth checking whether you will be able to pay extra for a room on your own or whether you will automatically be expected to share with someone else. You have to decide how much you value your privacy – a single room supplement, if available, can add at least £25 a week to the cost of your holiday.

If a beach-based holiday is not really your ideal break you could always consider an *adventure holiday*. Ask your travel agent or study the holiday advertisements in the Sunday papers. There is a wide range to choose from, particularly if money is not a problem. You could go on a wildlife safari to Africa, trek into the remote parts of Tibet, go bird-watching in Iceland, temple visiting in Thailand.

Or what about a holiday that also teaches you a new *sport?* You could learn to windsurf in the Med, go flotilla sailing in Greece, be taught tennis or golf in the Algarve. You do not have to go abroad, however, to find an activity or hobby to follow on your holiday. The English Tourist Board actually publishes a book called *Activity and Hobby Holidays* which lists hundreds of holidays with a difference. The book is divided into sections covering action and sports, arts and crafts, and special interests. The range is enormous, from archery to squash, brass rubbing to film making, tracing your ancestors to beekeeping.

The courses are all residential. Accommodation varies – sometimes you are based in special centres, in schools, colleges or hotels and guest houses. Each entry in the book also makes it clear if singles are particularly welcome. There is also a choice between weekend breaks, midweek short courses and holidays of a week or more.

You can improve your mind by going on a philosophy course or your palate by taking a wine weekend break. And if you feel you need a holiday to get you back in shape there are plenty of places offering keep-fit, yoga or beauty care.

If you are a single parent you might be interested in sharing an activity holiday with your children. Certainly if you have older children it would be possible to take them pony trekking or painting, cycling or learning about computers. The book also lists a wide variety of holidays for children – so you could send them off to follow their interests while you did something else.

One company which specializes in holidays for one-parent families both in Britain and abroad is Gingerbread Holidays. There is a range of popular holiday resorts to choose from – places like Hayling Island, Scarborough, and Barry Island in Britain and Torremolinos in Spain – and the accommodation offered varies from caravans, chalets and guest houses to hotels. The company also organizes children-only holidays, including a farm holiday for six to nine year olds and a Midlands canal cruise for thirteen to fifteen year olds.

### Checking the details

Once you have selected a holiday that sounds as if it might suit you, there are other steps you can take to make sure you enjoy it to the full. Whether you plan to stay in Britain or go abroad, it pays to read the literature or the holiday brochure very carefully before you book. Even a weekend break in the Cotswolds can be spoiled, for example, if you discover on arrival that the charming little hotel miles from anywhere has no bar, or that there is only one bathroom shared between eight bedrooms.

It can be even worse to discover that your holiday hotel in Spain is right under the flight path of the neighbouring airport when you had hoped for two weeks' peace and quiet, or that the nearest beach is a good two miles' trek away.

Learn to read between the lines. A purpose built complex means modern hotels and apartments probably miles from any genuine local colour in the form of shops, bars or restaurants. Watch out for words like 'lively', 'bustling', or 'in the heart of things': they can be euphemisms for noisy. On the other hand, 'totally relaxing', 'a place to unwind', 'get-away-from-it-all' can mean dead as a dodo after the sun goes down, isolated, miles from anywhere.

If you are planning to go anywhere out of the high season check first to make sure which facilities will be available. Will the hotel disco be open? Will the swimming pool be in use? Will the local bars have opened for business?

It may be worth asking your travel agent if he has a copy of *The Agent's Hotel Gazetteer* (C.H.G. Travel Publications). This is published for the trade and gives an independent assessment of most of the major holiday resorts abroad, warts and all, as well as details for many of the hotels featured in the brochures. And if you are going abroad is it worth checking whether the company you are booking with is a member of ABTA (The Association of British Travel Agents) as this will give you greater consumer protection in case anything goes wrong.

It is also important before you set off on holiday, however hard you are trying to keep costs down, to take out adequate insurance to cover problems like falling ill, losing your luggage, having to cancel at the last minute and so on. You can either choose to get cover from a 'holiday insurance package policy' or by a 'selective holiday policy'. You do not have to go for the policy your travel company suggests – a selective policy, for instance, allows you to buy increased sums insured for some risks and to ignore others. Ask your travel agent for advice.

A typical package policy will cost around £10 for a fortnight's cover in Europe and the Mediterranean area. Premiums are usually higher for places further afield, including the USA. The sort of cover you might get for your premium should include:

*Property*:    Up to £1,000 for loss of or damage to baggage, clothing and personal effects. There is usually a limit of £200 to £250 for lost money, travellers cheques etc. and a single item limit of £150 to £250. Losses must usually be reported to the local police within twenty-four hours and proof of this notification will be needed when you make a claim.

*Personal accident*:    Benefits are usually payable on death, disablement, loss of eyes or limb. Usual cover up to £15,000.

*Personal liability*:    This covers your legal liability for injury or damage which you may cause to others and their property. Usual cover £250,000 to £500,000.

*Cancellation or curtailment*:    This cover can be useful if you have to cancel or cut short your holiday because of unforeseen circumstances such as accident or illness, jury service or witness summons. Some policies also include cover for cancellation arising from strike, or adverse weather conditions affecting departure. Usual cover £500 to £1,000.

*Delay*:    Some policies pay compensation if the start of your holiday is delayed beyond a certain time as a direct result of strikes, industrial action, adverse weather or mechanical breakdown. There is usually a limit – perhaps £90 maximum or up to the holiday cost if you decide to cancel your holiday after the first twelve hours.

*Medical expenses*:     As well as covering the cost of aid or treatment, cover is usually provided for additional hotel expenses and travel expenses related to sickness or injury and expenses incurred in returning home. The cover varies considerably from package to package but can be as much as £100,000.

It it worth taking out holiday insurance for medical cover alone. However firmly you believe you will not fall ill or be involved in an accident on holiday, do not kid yourself. It could happen to you and, however much we knock the NHS, Britain still has a health service way ahead of much of the rest of the world.

Even if you are taking a holiday in an EEC country or in a country which has a reciprocal health care arrangement with Britain, most of these countries do not offer a comprehensive health care service. Medical treatment abroad can be very expensive – treatment for a serious accident or illness could cost thousands of pounds and even a minor ailment could be expensive. And the cost of repatriation is never covered by any arrangement between countries.

In Greece, for example, people seeking treatment under the Greek Social Insurance Scheme (IKA) often have long waits for attention both in local IKA offices and surgeries/hospitals. Hospital wards are likely to be crowded and may not give all the services usual in other Community countries. You would be better off seeking private treatment.

A leaflet, available from your local DHSS office explains what is available where, and how to go about getting: SA30, 'Medical Costs Abroad – what you need to know before you go'. In the EEC you may need a certificate of entitlement (Form E111) to get free or reduced-cost treatment in an emergency. You can apply for this by filling in the form at the back of leaflet SA30 between one and six months before you plan to go away.

Another useful leaflet published by the DHSS lists all the vaccinations and health risks you need to be aware of when travelling abroad – SA35, 'Protect your health abroad'. Obviously, the more exotic your holiday destination, the more likely you are to need protection against cholera, yellow fever, malaria or infectious hepatitis. But even if you are going to a less out of the way spot like the South of France or a Greek island you may well be advised to be vaccinated against polio, tetanus and typhoid. Check with your own doctor and the checklist in the leaflet, but remember to do this in plenty of time. Vaccination against polio, for instance, involves three doses of drops from your doctor, taken at four to eight week intervals.

Travelling can be fun or it can be a chore. There are some tips you can follow, though, which should take some of the pain out of getting away, even if they cannot always guarantee it will be a pleasure:

*Be ruthless when you are packing.* There will always be some point in your journey when you are going to have to carry – by yourself – all your luggage. And if that consists of one large suitcase, one small one, a carrier bag of dutyfrees, a handbag and a shoulder bag, that will be no joke.

*Have some food and drink to hand.* There is nothing worse than being stuck in a motorway jam or an airport lounge when all the bars and restaurants are closed and you are dying of hunger and thirst. A carton of juice and a small packet of biscuits could feel like a lifesaver.

*Put comfort before high fashion.* It may be tempting to wear your newly bought outfit to travel in, but what you really need is something loose fitting. Low-heeled comfortable shoes are best, too, as feet tend to swell if you sit still for too long. Go for layers you can peel off or put on as the temperature changes and forget all-in-one flying suits/dungarees etc. (Struggling in and out of them in motorway/aircraft loos etc. needs the skill of a contortionist.)

*Avoid cigarettes and alcohol if you are flying.* The air in aircraft cabins is slightly thinner than at sea level and dryer because of the air conditioning, so smoking will give you a headache and alcohol will make you dehydrate even more. Instead, drink plenty of water or non-alcoholic drinks before and during the flight.

*Spot your case*. One suitcase looks very like another in the baggage reclaim area. Make yours easier to spot by putting special stickers on it. That way you will not find yourself unpacking someone else's luggage when you get to your hotel.

The best piece of advice worth taking, however, is simple: *don't overdo things*. There is a temptation to rush out into the sun and spend all day on the beach, then rave it up at night eating and drinking. But that is a surefire way to ruin the rest of your precious two weeks.

Skin specialists point out that a tan is actually a sign that the skin has been damaged – however much the rest of us like to think of a tan as 'healthy'. So take it easy. Use a sunscreen with a fairly high protection factor at first and do not sunbathe between noon and 2 p.m. unless you want to get burnt. Some medicines – including the contraceptive Pill – can make the skin more sensitive to sunlight, as can some cosmetics, perfumes and deodorant soaps.

Soothe sunburn with a lotion containing calamine and if you start to run a temperature and feel ill, sponge yourself with cold water and take a couple of aspirin. If you are badly burnt, seek medical attention.

In hot climates you need to drink plenty of fluids – but this does not mean lots of alcohol! It is a good idea to stick to bottled, boiled or sterilized water for drinking, teeth cleaning, mouth washing and so on, but it does seem rather crazy to blame the water you had in your umpteen scotches or the ice in your half dozen rum and cokes for every case of Montezuma's revenge the following day. And there is no point being fanatical about the local water if you do not take as much care about what you eat. Be wary of cream, ice cream, raw vegetables, salads and unpeeled fruit. Seafood is a notorious hazard. Watch out for underdone or reheated meat or fish.

If, despite all your care, you still seem to be spending more time in the loo than on the beach, what should you do? In itself diarrhoea is not dangerous – but the dehydration it causes can be. So you must keep up your fluid intake. You could try a mixture of one level 5 ml teaspoon salt, with eight level spoons of sugar in at least a litre of drinking water, drunk little and often.

If you want to take some kind of medicine it is best to stick to a simple solution of kaolin and morphine but if the attack goes on for more than forty-eight hours consult a doctor just in case it is more serious than an upset stomach.

One thing to bear in mind is the fact that any medicines you were already taking may not be completely absorbed – and that includes the Pill. So you may need some other form of birth control for the rest of the month or cycle.

## Useful addresses and phone numbers

Small World:    850 Brighton Road, Purley, Surrey, CR2 2BH, 01-660 3999.

Young World:    29 Queens Road, Brighton BN1 3YN, 0273 202391.

Singles Holidays:    The Agora, 10-23 Church Street, Wolverton, Milton Keynes MK12 5LG, 0908 318783.

English Tourist Board:    4 Grosvenor Gardens, London SW1W 0DU, 01-730 3400. (Their publication, *Activity and Hobby Holidays in England*, is also available through bookshops, newsagents, and a number of Tourist Information Centres.)

City and Guilds of London Leisure Courses:    46, Britannia Street London WC1 01-278 2468

YHA Adventure Holidays:    YHA Travel, 14 Southampton Street, London WC2E 7HY, 01-240 5236.

The Association of British Craftsmen:    57 Coombe Bridge Avenue, Stoke Bishop, Bristol, Avon BS9 2LT, 0272 686417. (Information about residential craft courses in the homes and studios of its members.)

For up-to-date information about vaccination requirements:
*England*:    International Relations Division, DHSS, Alexander Fleming House, London SE1 6BY, 01-407 5522, ext 6749.
or
Public Health Laboratory Service, Communicable Disease

Surveillance Centre, 61 Colindale Avenue, London NW9 5EQ, 01-200 6868.

*Scotland*:    Scottish Home and Health Department, St Andrew's House, Edinburgh EH1 3DE, 031-5568501, ext 2438.

or

The Communicable Diseases (Scotland) Unit, Ruchill Hospital, Bilsland Drive, Glasgow G20 9NB, 041 9467120.

*Wales*:    Welsh Office, Cathays Park, Cardiff CF1 3NQ, 0222 825111, ext 3395.

*Northern Ireland*:    DHSS, Dundonald House, Upper Newtownards Rd, Belfast BT4 3SF, 0232 63939, ext 2593.

# 10
# The Single Woman Staying Healthy

These days no one assumes that good health is simply a matter of luck. We know that the way we live – from the food we eat to the stress we work under – can affect the way we feel and the shape our bodies are in. Slowly, but surely, the emphasis is swinging away from simply finding cures for illness to ways of preventing illness in the first place. And this means that there are lots of steps a woman can take to make sure she is fit and healthy enough to enjoy the pleasures of being single.

## Your doctor

Nevertheless, there are still times when every woman will need to see a doctor. So how do you go about finding a GP – or changing doctors if you do not get on with the one you have? If you have moved it is best not to wait until you need a doctor before trying to find one. A complete list of NHS doctors in your area, and their surgery hours, can be obtained from your Family Practitioner Committee whose address is on your medical card. A list will probably also be available in the post office, library and citizens' advice bureau.

Ask around to see what others living in your area think about their doctors. Some may have a reputation for being particularly understanding of women's health problems – pre-menstrual tension, for instance. Others may be good with children.

Try to find out how easy it is to see a doctor in a hurry or whether he/she operates a fairly rigid appointments system. Once you have made some basic inquiries you will have to find out whether the doctor of your choice will accept you. You may find his lists are full, so phone to check first. Once you have found a doctor, simply fill in Part A on your medical card and give this to your new doctor who will sign Part A and then send the card off to the FPC for registration. The FPC will eventually send you a new card.

If you want to change your doctor for any other reason than a change of address there are two ways of doing this. One involves getting the consent of your doctor, the other does not.

1.  Ask your present doctor for his consent to transfer to the doctor of your choice (you can do this in writing, if you prefer). If he agrees, you ask him to sign Part B of your medical card, then you and the new doctor complete Part A as above.

2.  If your present doctor refuses to release you, or if you do not want to ask him directly for his consent, you can send your medical card direct to the FPC with a letter saying you want to transfer to Dr So-and-so. You do not have to give a reason, though you can if you wish to. You will get your card back with a slip stuck in it giving you permission to transfer after a given date (fourteen days after the FPC received your application). This slip is valid for one month and if you stick with your decision to change doctors you must, within this time, complete Part 1 of the transfer slip and take or send it with your card to the new doctor. If he accepts you he signs Part 2 of the slip and you are then on his list. You will be sent a new medical card later.

Sometimes doctors are reluctant to accept patients who want to transfer from another doctor's list in the same area, particularly if they feel it may be seen as 'poaching'. If you cannot find any doctor who will accept you, you can write to the FPC asking them to assign you to a doctor, but you must first do the rounds of trying to find another doctor yourself. When you write to the FPC, tell them the name or names of doctors who have refused you and of any doctors with whom you would prefer not to be registered.

In an emergency, if you are without a doctor, or your own doctor is not available, you are entitled to treatment from any available doctor in the district. And if you are away from home for three months or less you can apply to a doctor for acceptance as a temporary patient. If you are a student living away from home and there is a health centre at your college or university, you may choose to register with a doctor at the health centre, but you can choose any other doctor in the area if you prefer.

If you have any problems with doctors or the health service in general you may be able to get help and advice from the Patients Association. Among their publications is a useful guide to some of the lesser known services and concessions of the health service and a guide to patients' legal rights.

## Physical check-ups

You may feel it is all right to go to your doctor if you have a sore throat or because you suffer from asthma, but not just because you would like a check-up. It seems crazy, but lots of women who would never dream of skipping the 5,000 mile service for their cars, for instance, are far more lax when it comes to their own body maintenance.

However, many GPs are interested in the whole area of preventative medicine and many now offer check-up services including advice on diet, blood-pressure readings, breast checks and cervical smears. There may be notices informing you of these services in your GP's surgery. In addition, if you go to your GP for contraceptive advice he should arrange for breast checks and cervical smears as a matter of routine. The same applies if you see a doctor at a family planning clinic.

There are also a number of private 'well woman' clinics dotted around the country. At Marie Stopes House in London, for example, a service called Medicheck is on offer for £40, which provides a full medical check-up specifically for women. BUPA also carries out health screening, both for women covered by BUPA health insurance and those who are not.

There are BUPA Medical Centres in London, Birmingham, Bristol, Cardiff, Glasgow, Manchester, Nottingham and Norwich. The services they offer are comprehensive, but not cheap. Full health screening with a physical examination and consultation with a doctor, for instance, takes three hours. Apart from taking a detailed personal, occupational, environmental and clinical history, you will have your hearing, vision and lung function tested. An electrocardiogram will give information about the condition of your heart: blood tests will check for liver, kidney and metabolic disease. You would also be given the Well Woman Screen, designed to identify breast and gynaecological diseases. You would be given a breast examination, including X-ray where indicated, a urine test and a pelvic examination.

For women not covered by BUPA health insurance prices range from £182 for the full health screening with doctor consultation to £64 for a Well Woman Screen alone.

The importance of checking regularly for any early warning signs of breast or cervical cancer cannot be underestimated. Recent statistics show that nine out of ten British women who died of cancer of the cervix had not had a smear test. One woman in twenty may develop breast cancer in their lifetime and each year 12,000 deaths from breast cancer are recorded in Britain.

Yet experts believe that most of the 2,000 deaths a year from cervical cancer could have been prevented if the women had been properly screened, and early treatment of breast cancer – whether by drugs, radiotherapy or surgery – may be 100 per cent effective.

Cervical screening, by means of smear tests, can detect any abnormalities in the cells of the cervix long before they become cancerous. Such cells can then be destroyed or removed and the cancer never has a chance to develop. Cervical smear tests involve an internal examination but they are quick and painless. The doctor gently inserts an instrument called a speculum into your vagina; then, using a wooden or metal spatula, scrapes a few cells from the outside of your cervix. These cells are transferred to a glass slide and sent off to a laboratory for miscroscopic examination. The results usually come back within two to six weeks.

Sometimes doctors ask you to ring up for your results: sometimes they tell you you will be contacted only if there is some indication of abnormality. But do not panic if you are asked to go back – the lab technicians can also spot other conditions like thrush, which may need treatment, or there may simply have been a technical problem in processing your slide.

The test can detect differing stages of abnormality in the cells, all of them pre-cancerous. When there is only a slight abnormality, the situation often reverses itself without any treatment and in this kind of situation you many simply be asked to return for more frequent checks so that the doctor can keep an eye on what is going on. If the doctor decides treatment is needed you may be admitted to hospital for a few days so that the suspect cells can be removed.

The operation, under a general anaesthetic, can be done in one of three ways:

*a cone biopsy* – a tiny, cone-shaped piece of tissue is surgically removed from the cervix,
*cryocautery* – carbon dioxide destroys the cells by freezing them,
*electrodiathermy* – heat is used to burn away the cells.

There is a newer technique, not so widely available, which can be carried out under a local anaesthetic as out-patient treatment, using a laser to make the cells evaporate. This need only take about twenty minutes.

Experts differ in their view of how often a woman should have a smear test done. The Department of Health guidelines suggest a new test every five years, but many women and doctors feel that the gap between tests should be no more than three years. As a general rule, though, a woman should have her first test done when she becomes sexually active, another a year later and regularly from then on until she is at least 65.

If you do not know whether you have been given a test recently – at your family planning clinic or ante-natal clinic, for instance – then ask. It will be on your notes.

The Women's National Cancer Control Campaign was formed in 1965 to help women overcome their fears about cancer and to take simple precautions which could well save their lives. They are concerned that out of a potential seventeen and a half million women, only two to three million are having regular cervical smears.

In fact, some women run more of a risk of getting cervical cancer than others. You are more likely to be in a high-risk category if you:

—started to have sexual relationships at an early age,

—have had a number of different sexual partners,

—have a partner who has had lots of other partners,

—have had any kind of sexually transmitted disease, especially herpes.

There is also some evidence that cervical cancer is more common in women who smoke heavily and one recent study suggested a link between long-term use of oral contraceptives and cancer of the cervix, but many medical experts have challenged this conclusion. The WNCCC suggest that if you feel you are in a particularly high-risk category you should mention this to your doctor who may feel it is necessary to monitor you more closely.

You do not have to go to a clinic or a doctor to have your breasts checked; you can do this yourself. Although breast cancer is pretty rare for some women under thirty, it is worth getting into the routine as soon as you can. The best time is probably a couple of days after your period has finished each month.

First you look, then you feel. You are *looking* for any changes – swelling, dimpling, puckering. Have your nipples turned in or are they pointing in a different direction? You are *feeling* for any lumps or thickening, not just in your breast but where it tails into your armpit.

LOOK:    Start by standing, arms at your sides, and just looking at your breasts in a mirror. Turn from side to side so you can see them from all angles. Then put your hands on your head and look again for anything unusual, particularly around the nipples. Stretch, arms above your head, and look again before finally bringing your hand on to your hips and pressing inwards so that your chest muscles tighten. Keep looking, especially for any dimpling.

FEEL:    Lie flat with your head on a pillow and your left shoulder raised by a folded towel. Feel your left breast with your right hand, using the flat of your fingers and keeping them together. Keep your left arm down at first and press your breast gently but firmly in towards your body. Work in a spiral, circling out from the nipple and make sure you feel every part. Then put your left arm over your head, with the elbow bent and repeat the spiral, feeling the outer part of the breast in particular. Finish by feeling where the breast tails off into the armpit. Then put the towel under your right shoulder and examine your right breast in the same way.

If you think you have found a lump or some other abnormality do not assume it is cancer. Eight out of tem lumps turn out to be something else – blocked milk ducts, cysts or mastitis, for example. Go to your doctor – he has far more experience and will be able to tell a lot more from palpating your breasts than you can. If he feels he needs more information he will probably refer you to your local hospital where you may be given a breast X-ray or scan. If there is any possibility that the lump might be malignant you will be admitted for two or three days so that it can be removed under a general anaesthetic and examined under a microscope.

Even if it *is* diagnosed as breast cancer, there is a good chance that treatment will be successful if the diagnosis is made early enough. Unlike cervical cancer, breast cancer does not have a warning, pre-cancerous phase. That is why early detection is so vital. And that is why it is worth carrying out those regular DIY breast checks.

## Smoking

Starting to have regular check-ups is one way of staying healthy, but stopping habits which can be harmful to health is just as important. After all, what is the point of religiously checking your body for signs of breast cancer if you are smoking yourself to death?

In 1982, lung cancer caused the deaths of 10,249 women in the United Kingdom. (Ninety per cent of lung cancers are caused by smoking.) Coronary heart disease is the most common cause of death in Britain. It used to be rare for women to have heart attacks, and it still is for women under 55 – who do not smoke.

Women who take the Pill and who also smoke cigarettes are more likely to have a heart attack, a stroke or a blood clot in the leg veins, which may shift to the lung, than non-smokers who are also on the Pill.

Giving up cigarettes may not be as hard as you think. Some

surveys show that over 65 per cent of ex-smokers say that stopping was suprisingly easy. Although some people swear that acupuncture or hypnotherapy worked for them, there is no 'miracle cure' for smoking. The main thing is that you should really want to quit. However, the Health Education Council has produced a leaflet, *So You Want To Stop Smoking*, which is full of useful tips.

Smokers smoke a lot of cigarettes out of sheer habit. Maybe they light up automatically after breakfast or when they have a cup of coffee. Sometimes they reach for their cigarettes when they pick up the phone, put a clean piece of paper in the typewriter, or when they turn on the television.

One way of breaking this kind of habit smoking is to change your routine. For instance, if you normally smoke after a meal get up straightaway instead, even if it is only to do the washing-up. Or keep a pen and pad handy by the phone and train yourself to doodle rather than smoke.

Another tip is to plan some new activities to replace smoking – things to distract yourself, things to do with your hands and different ways to cope with tension. Some people find it helps to knit, or play with a bunch of keys or worry beads. Others chew gum or matches.

Enlist the help of your friends and family. Maybe you could agree to stop smoking at the same time as someone else. Or get someone to sponsor you to stop. Or make a bet with someone that you will stop for so long – say three months.

Some people find it helps to cut down on the number of cigarettes they smoke before they actually give up. But the danger of doing this is that you can simply go on putting off the evil day and eventually find yourself smoking as much as ever.

Remind yourself of the advantages of not smoking – more money to spend on other things, no more bad breath, stained fingers or teeth, being able to run up stairs without getting out of breath, winters of fewer colds and other infections and, of course, a better life expectancy. Then, when you have made up your mind, pick on a day when you will not be under much stress. The day before, get rid of all your cigarettes, ashtrays and lighters. Then take it one day at a time. Make the first day special. Treat yourself to a lie-in or a long, lazy bath. Have fruit juice for breakfast. The taste is fresh and the acidity helps get rid of the nicotine. Give yourself a treat at the end of the day as a reward for not smoking.

You may not find the process as tough as you anticipated. But at first you may be irritable and find it hard to concentrate. You may find your mood swings wildly – happy one minute, depressed the next. You may even feel more ill to start with – as the cleaning action in your lungs gets started, for instance, you may develop a bad cough. But all these side-effects are part of the process of getting better and free from the constant supply of nicotine your body is used to. They should pass in a few weeks.

Once you have stopped, keep at it. If people offer you cigarettes do not say you have given up, tell them *you do not smoke*. They will stop offering them and that will be one temptation less.

Some women find it helps to save up the money they would have been spending on cigarettes so they can treat themselves from time to time as a reward for not smoking. Another idea is to keep busy or to spend more times in places where you would not have smoked in the past. One girl I know never smoked in the bathroom or the bedroom, although she managed to get through twenty-a-day smoking just about everywhere else. She took to watching TV in bed instead of in the living room and she spent so much time in the bath she could easily have won the title for the cleanest girl in North London. *But she managed to stop smoking.*

No one can tell you how long it will be before you stop wanting cigarettes. For some people the craving vanishes after a few days. For others it may take weeks or even years. The danger is that you will think, after a while, that it will not hurt to have the occasional cigarette.

The fact is, it probably will. It is all too easy to slip gradually back into your old habits until you find you are smoking as many, if not more, than before. Most smokers will admit, if asked, that they have 'given up' at least once in their lives. But if you do start smoking again it does not mean you are a failure. Learn from what went wrong and pick another day to stop again. As the Health

Education Council leaflet points out, you may have lost the battle, but you can still win the war.

Apart from all the other risks of smoking, there is some evidence to suggest that smokers may be less able to absorb Vitamin C from their diet than non-smokers. Alcohol, too, may deplete the body of certain vitamins, particularly those in the B range. On top of that, drink can suppress your appetite so that you are not eating sensibly in the first place.

## Drinking

These days more and more women drink alcohol. Supermarkets sell a whole range of drinks along with the frozen foods and the corn flakes. Wine bars have replaced coffee shops as the smart places to meet your girl friends, and even pubs are trying to woo single women over the threshold. But, however socially acceptable it now is for a woman to be seen with a glass in her hand, women cannot safely drink as much as men. Even 'social' drinking can be a danger to your health.

Studies have shown that women, because they are generally smaller and lighter than men, are more susceptible to alcohol-related health problems such as cirrhosis of the liver. They also tend to develop dependence on alcohol more quickly. In addition, drinking during pregnancy can damage the unborn child.

It is now generally accepted that while men can safely consume up to 20 units of alcohol a week, a woman's limit should be 13. A unit is 8-10 grams of pure alcohol – or half a pint of beer, a glass of wine (table or fortified), or a single measure of spirits.

One way of cutting down on your drinking, if you do not want to stop altogether, is to keep a weekly diary. Jot down the number of units you drink each day and work out ways to reduce the number. Most wine bars, for instance, sell mineral water as well as wine. Even if you do not want to spend a whole lunch time sipping water, you can water down a glass of wine and make it last twice as long.

In pubs you do not have to switch to slim-line tonics or fruit juices, though many women find them useful alternatives to alcohol. There are now alcohol-free beers on sale and another refreshing drink that most pubs will serve is lemonade and lime.

At parties, if you want to avoid the kind of people who cannot bear to see others being teetotal while they are swigging back the booze as if there is no tomorrow, try putting ice in a glass of dry ginger – it looks just like scotch and dry. Or a twist of lemon in a wine glass of lemonade – who is to know there is no vermouth in there?

Learn to sip your drinks. If you are having wine with a meal, then ask for a jug of water as well. Do not use alcohol to quench your thirst. And do not succumb to pressure from others to get you to drink more than you want to. Sometimes it can be hard to turn down the offer of a drink, but you do not have to give excuses or explanations – nor do you have to launch into a lecture on the evils of alcohol! However, if you do feel the need of a handy excuse or two you could always try:

—'I'm on a diet.'
—'I've got a bet with a friend to see who can cut out drink the longest.'
—'I'm allergic to alcohol.'

One of the problems single women sometimes face is that when they go to the pub they want to be 'one of the boys' and this can mean getting involved in buying rounds of drinks. It also means you get bought far more individual drinks than you would have bought for yourself. You can avoid this without seeming a killjoy if you plead poverty, but still stick to your independence. Say you cannot afford to get caught up in the round and, just this once, you will buy your own.

## Eating sensibly

Cutting out cigarettes and cutting down on alcohol are two of the things you can do to stay healthier. Eating properly is another. The problem is, it is hard to have a balanced attitude to food. From childhood we learn to see certain types of food as rewards for good behaviour. We use food for comfort; we go out to eat to celebrate; we cook meals to show others how much we like or care for them. In other words, food is far more than fuel for our bodies.

At the same time we are constantly bombarded with the message that thin is beautiful. There are magazines on the newstands filled with nothing but diets and slimming tips. Chemists' shelves groan under the weight of slimming aids and slimmers' meals. Small wonder that so many single women seem to spend their lives see-sawing between going out for lavish dinner parties or restaurant meals and then spending the next week on an 800-calorie a day crash diet. And small wonder that some women become so obsessed with dieting that they develop anorexia nervosa or become 'binge' eaters, stuffing themselves with food one minute, then forcing themselves to be sick the next.

If you have any reason to believe your eating habits have become really out of hand you should seek medical help. One organization which also offers support is Anorexic Aid (see the list of addresses at the end of this chapter). A network of self-help groups operate up and down the country, whereby anorexics share their problems and learn how others have managed to overcome them.

Diets and dieting are big business. So if you *do* decide you want to lose weight, what is the best way to go about it? *Which? Way to Slim*, published by the Consumers Association provides a very thorough run-down on many of the ways people try to diet, from counting calories, cutting down on carbohydrates, to going to health farms and joining slimming clubs. They also carried out a survey of women who were or had been trying to slim. The survey showed that for a long-term weight loss, belonging to a slimming group got the women's top vote (51 per cent), followed by diet alone (41 per cent) and diet plus increased exercise (40 per cent). But younger women tended to go for a method which combined exercise and diet, while older women were keener on dieting only or dieting with a group.

Another interesting book – and one which has been described as an anti-diet book – is Susie Orbach's *Fat is a Feminist Issue* (published by Hamlyn paperbacks). The idea behind the book is that women can learn through case histories and a series of simple exercises, how to break the binge-diet-binge syndrome and help their bodies to find and stay at their natural weight.

Whatever your views are about dieting, there is no doubt that being fat is a danger to your health. The fatter you are, the greater your chance of dying at an early age. Fat people are more likely to suffer from diabetes, high blood-pressure, and disease of the arteries of the heart, which can lead to strokes or heart attacks. If you are overweight you are also more likely to suffer from arthritis of the knees or the hips or from gall bladder disease.

And even if you are not fat, you could still be eating too much of the kind of food which does little to contribute to better health.

Most of us eat too much fat and sugar – both linked with heart disease by doctors. The annual sugar consumption, for instance, is around 43 kg per person. It sounds staggering, but sugar is added to so many products, as you can see if you read the labels on the foods in your own larder. At the same time, we tend not to eat enough fibre and even if we *do* eat fresh fruit and vegetables, we often destroy the vitamins by over cooking.

Here are some tips for healthier eating:

—Trim all visible fat off meat and go for chicken or turkey, or offal rather than beef, lamb or pork.
—Grill rather than fry.
—Use foil or roasting bags for roasting or baking so you do not need to use extra fat.
—Buy tinned fish in brine not oil.
—Avoid cream – try natural yogurt instead.
— Cut down your hard cheese intake – go for Edam instead of Cheddar.
—Use skimmed milk instead of full-cream milk.
—If you must fry use non-stick pans and a pastry brush for the smallest amount of fat.
—Use vegetable purées to thicken sauces and soups instead of fat and flour.
—Dress salads with lemon juice instead of oil and vinegar.
—Buy tinned fruit in natural juice, not syrup.
—Buy wholemeal bread and pasta.
—Eat jacket potatoes instead of chips.
—Choose a bran breakfast cereal.

—Use vegetables as cases for meat instead of pastry – stuffed cabbage leaves, stuffed marrow etc.

—Do not peel apples, pears etc.

—Use low-fat spreads where possible, not butter.

A healthy diet is one which contains a balance of protein, fat, carbohydrate, minerals, vitamins and roughage. We need protein for growth and tissue repair; fat for energy and essential fatty acids; carbohydrates for energy; and vitamins and minerals to help the body's metabolism to work properly. When you are single it is all too easy to skip meals, to fill up on fast-food snacks, to raid the biscuit jar because you cannot be bothered to cook for one. But to stay healthily single it is worth taking a little time to put your eating habits on the right track. Most doctors and nutritionists feel that if you are eating properly you do not need extra vitamins or minerals in the form of pills or supplements. But if you are not, you may find it worth the money taking multivitamin tablets or a combination of supplements. A good multivitamin tablet should contain vitamins, A, D, the B complex, C and a selection of minerals.

**Exercise**

Just as slimming and the whole question of diet has become big business, so, too, has the flipside of the coin – exercise. Of course, staying trim and keeping fit will help you look and feel better but there is no need to push yourself to painful limits or spend a fortune to do this.

There are fashions in keeping fit, just as there are fashions in everything else. A few years ago jogging was the 'in' thing, then came aerobics. The latest trend seems to be weight training for women. One of the dangers of following fads is that there are always bound to be inexperienced people ready to jump on the bandwagon and start classes in whatever is currently fashionable, with little or no training or qualifications of their own. And, if you are not careful, far from getting fitter you may simply overdo it.

Take aerobic exercise, for instance. Aerobic simply means 'with air' and so can be used to refer to any exercise which is highly active and increases the body's demand for oxygen. Aerobic exercise improves the efficiency of the heart and lungs and increases the body's *stamina*.

However, this is just one way in which exercise can affect your body. Other types of exercise can primarily increase your *strength* or your *suppleness*.

So, apart from exercising regularly, it is a good idea to vary the type of exercise you take if you want to improve the level of your overall fitness. Yoga, for instance, is good for improving your body's flexibility, while working out with weights will do wonders for your strength.

You do not have to jog or go to classes to take aerobic exercise. *Brisk* walking for at least twenty minutes has the same effect, as does continuous disco dancing or cycling. You do not even have to go outdoors: buy yourself an exercise bike or dance to disco records on your stereo. And it is worth knowing that the best overall exercise is swimming.

However, to get fit, it is no use going at it half-heartedly. You will need a minimum of three 20 to 30-minute workouts a week. And you cannot get fit unless you put a certain amount of effort into it. But do take things carefully at first. Build up slowly and consult your doctor if you have high blood-pressure, a heart condition or any kind of back problem *before* you get carried away by any vigorous exercise plan.

Instead of wearing you out, regular exercise can make you feel as if you have more energy to go round. Another way of tapping your energy reserves is to learn how to relax. Stress is one of the bugbears of modern life and single women have to cope with their share of it. Stress can cause all kinds of physical problems from headaches, insomnia, indigestion and palpitations. When we are under stress our bodies tend to tense up: learning how to relax and release that tension will not only make you feel better, it will enable you to handle problems better too.

One way of relaxing is to lie down in a quiet, dimly lit room, flat on your back with your legs slightly apart and your hands, palms up, by your sides. Close your eyes. Then, starting with your toes and your feet, deliberately tense the muscles in each part of your body in turn, then let them relax. Gradually work all the way up to your scalp, not forgetting the muscles of your pelvic floor and your mouth.

When you are completely relaxed just concentrate on listening to the pattern of your breathing, without disturbing it and try to let your mind go as limp as your body. Think of the tension draining out of your body, into the floor. Imagine yourself getting heavier and heavier.

If you practise this tense-relax technique once a day for fifteen minutes you should soon be able to relax any time, anywhere, without having to run through the tension exercises first.

Learn to watch out for signs of tension during the day. Remember to relax your shoulders when you are driving. Use traffic jams as a chance to practise breathing slowly and calmly. If you are up against a deadline at work or facing a confrontation with the boss, check the tension in your hands and your face. Let your hands go limp in your lap. Stop gritting your teeth!

Never feel guilty about taking time to relax, however hectic your daily schedule may be. It gives you greater energy in the end and can help you enjoy doing both the things you have to do and the things you want to.

### Useful addressess and publications

The Patients Association:     Room 33, 18 Charing Cross Road, LondonWC2H 0HR, 01-240 0671.

Marie Stopes House:     108, Whitfield Street, London W1P 6BE, 01-388 0662/2585.

BUPA:   BUPA Medical centres are at the following addresses:
   London:    (Women's Unit) Battle Bridge House, 300 Gray's Inn Rd, London WC1X 8DU, 01-837 6484.
   Birmingham:    Unicorn House, 29 Smallbrook Queensway, Birmingham B5 4HE, 021-632 6738.
   Brentwood: Hartswood Hospital, Warley Road, Brentwood, Essex CM13 3HR, 0277 232525.
   Bristol:    Stafford Lodge, The Chesterfield Hospital, Clifton Hill, Bristol BS8 1BP, 0272 731433.

Cardiff:    BUPA Hospital Cardiff, Croescadarn Rd, Pentwyn, CF2 7XL, 0222 735515.

Glasgow:    Axton House, 295 Fenwick Road, Giffnock, Glasgow G46 6UH. 041-638 4445.

Leeds: 81 Clarendon Road, Leeds LF2 9PJ, 0532 436735,

Manchester:    9 St John Street, Manchester M3 4DW, 061-833 9362.

Nottingham:    Clawson Lodge, 403 Mansfield Rd, Nottingham NG5 2DP, 0602 622826.

Norwich:    BUPA Hospital Norwich, Old Watton Rd, Colney, Norwich NR4 7TD, 0603 56181.

Women's National Cancer Control Campaign, 1 South Audley St, London W1Y 5DQ, 01-499 7532. (They publish a wide range of literature about cervical smears and breast self-examination.)

Health Education Council, 78 New Oxford Street, London WC1A 1AH, 01-637 1881. Publications include:
'Looking After Yourself'
'That's the Limit – a Guide to Sensible Drinking'
'Stay Fit in the Office'
'Fibre in Your Food'
'Fat – Who Needs It?'

The Scottish Health Education Group, Health Education Centre, Woodburn House, Canaan Lane, Edinburgh EH10 4SG, 031-447 8044.

ASH (Action on Smoking and Health), 5-11 Mortimer Street, London W1N 7RH, 01-637 9843.

Alcohol Concern, 3 Grosvenor Crescent, London SW1X 7EE, 01-235 4182. (They publish some useful literature including 'What Every Teenager Should Know About Alcohol' and 'Women and Alcohol'.)

Anorexic Aid, The Priory Centre, 11 Priory Road, High Wycombe, Bucks., 0494 21431 (24-hour answering machine).

# 11
# The Single Woman Staying Safe

There is nothing quite like that panicky moment when you are walking home from the bus stop late at night and you hear menacing footsteps following you. What should you do? Run? Scream? Pray? Turn round and knee the fellow where it hurts most?

Most single women have found themselves in situations where they have suddenly been scared stiff; scared of being mugged, beaten up, raped, even murdered.

Even what seemed to be safe can become threatening. You look up from the magazine you are reading on the last tube train home only to find there is no one left in the compartment except an odd-looking man.

You accept the offer of a lift home from a party from a guy who has been chatting you up – only to realize that he is taking the scenic route back.

You are driving home late from work when a carload of drunken teenagers starts following you.

Sometimes it seems as if the only way a single girl can stay safe is either to become a total recluse – or to turn into a kind of self-defence machine, equipped with anti-mugging devices, a black belt in karate and fists of steel.

It does not have to be like that, of course. There are lots of ways a girl can learn to be streetwise without spending hours or a small fortune taking martial arts courses. And, in any case, even some of the instructors who teach the variety of self-defence courses now available, are careful to stress that fighting back should generally be used as a last resort.

This is not to say that taking a self-defence course is a waste of time: for one thing, it is almost bound to make you fitter – and the fitter you are, the faster you can run! It may also give you confidence and there is something to be said for the theory that if you do not look like a victim, you will not become one. And if you *do* decide that hitting back is the way out of trouble, at least you should be able to hit back effectively.

On the other hand, taking a course may give you too much confidence. Whatever some people may believe, a 4 ft 11 in, 8 st girl is never going to flatten a 6 ft, 15 st man, and although looking as if you would be handy in a fight might deter the casual attacker, using violence against someone who has gone out looking for trouble could actually cost you your life.

Many self-defence courses are run by existing schools already teaching martial arts. Others have been set up to cash in on the recent interest from women who feel it is time they learnt how to fight back. Not all these instructors have training or qualifications, however, so it is best to check carefully before you part with your cash.

The Martial Arts Commission can give you information on self-defence classes in your area. Their own approved MAC1 self-defence system is available for instructors wanting to teach self-defence to amateurs.

Another tricky question is whether or not to carry anything with which to protect yourself or something to sound the alarm if you are attacked. If you carry a penknife, for example, or a bag of pepper to throw into an assailant's eyes, YOU could end up in court for carrying an offensive weapon. No one is going to prosecute you for carrying a whistle or an alarm – but can you guarantee you would have the puff to blow one or the time to set off the other – or that the great British public would take any notice if you did?

**Be prepared**

This is not meant to sound defeatist. If you would feel happier carrying something for your own defence it is worth knowing that perfume sprayed in someone's eyes is probably as painful as pepper, that the spike of an umbrella could be as effective as a penknife – and it is quite possible you would have both of these with you whether you felt there was any risk of attack or not.

Similarly, your front door keys could become a kind of knuckleduster, and a rolled up newspaper a kind of cosh. Even a handbag or case – or the stiletto heel on your shoe jabbed hard into a man's instep – could be enough of a weapon to give you time to run or get help.

My own feeling, though, is that this kind of hand-to-hand grappling is a last resort. The main thing is to avoid becoming a victim in the first place. In other words you have to learn to think ahead and be prepared.

If you are going out for the evening make sure beforehand that you know the times of the last bus/train/tube home. If you are driving, make sure the car is filled up with petrol, water, oil etc., so that you are unlikely to have any problems finding a filling station late at night. Make sure you have the phone number of a late-night cab service – and enough change for a call box. Take enough money to cover the cost of a cab if necessary. Even your bank manager could not be so hard hearted as to want you to walk home at 2 a.m. and risk your life simply to keep in the black!

Whenever possible let your parents, your flatmates, your babysitter, your best friend, your neighbours or whoever, know WHERE you are going, WHO you will be with, WHAT TIME you expect to be home.

If a man offers you a lift back from a dance, a disco or a party make sure someone else you know there knows who you are going with. Ask yourself if the risk is worth saving the price of a cab fare for, especially if you have been drinking (or if he has). Suggest he drops your friend off as well (if he is really keen on you he will not mind.)

## On the street
—There's safety in numbers – find another girl to walk home with if possible.
—Walk quickly and purposefully.

—Try to keep to well-lit streets and avoid side-roads and dark alleyways or open space.

—If you regularly walk home late from work, vary your route.

—Familiarize yourself with places of refuge – pubs, late-night shops etc.

—Know where the phone boxes are in case you need to call for help.

## On public transport

—Try to sit near couples or other women.

—Do not be afraid to pull the communication cord on a tube or train.

## In your car

—Lock the doors.

—Do not stop for hitch-hikers.

—If a man you are giving a lift to turns nasty try to attract attention – maybe you can switch off your lights at night or flash the headlight to alert police patrol cars.

—If you are being followed, drive to the nearest police station.

It is all very well for feminists to say that women should be free to dress and act as they please without being made to feel that they might be provoking an attack. But it seems, to me, naive to think you can wear an outfit to a disco to attract men and expect that same outfit to pass unnoticed in the street outside. Do not ask for trouble – cover up your more blatant charms.

Similarly, do not flash your cash – take only enough money to cover the costs of a night out, allowing for emergencies. And make sure it is in change and small notes. Why encourage strangers to think you might have a handbag full of tenners?

And, talking of handbags, do not leave yours lying around over the back of your chair in pubs or wine bars. Keep it on your lap. Do not let it hang from your shoulder or dangle by the strap in your hand when you are walking along the street. Hug it close to your body. Leave your credit cards at home unless you know you will need them.

If, despite all these precautions, you think you are being

followed then the main thing is not to let panic take over. That is often easier said than done, but it can help to take some deep breaths and count slowly under your breath. When you are in control, take action.

Do not be afraid of looking a fool. It is better to suffer a little embarrassment than an attack. Keep walking but start to make a lot of noise. Fire! is more likely to get a response than Help! or Rape! You could even try shouting at the man himself – 'Are you following me?'. Anything to create a scene and attract attention will do. Of course, if you are miles from anywhere and there is no one nearby, shouting or screaming will just sap your energy. Then you may as well save your breath.

Do not wait until it is too late to do anything simply because you are worried you might be making a mistake. If you are walking home in the dark and you are convinced the man behind is stalking you, make for a house where the lights are still on and ring the bell. Chances are that he will not follow you up the path.

Or get to a phone box and dial 999. Do not worry that you are being melodramatic. The police would rather you played safe than ended up being sorry. Other places of refuge might be a late-night supermarket or a pub. Do not be afraid to walk in and ask to use the phone. Call the police or ring for a cab.

If there are other people about you could always go up to them or call out to them. If you call 'Hello Grandad' to an elderly man your would-be attacker might think twice. Claiming a couple of older women as your aunties might give them a surprise, but they are fairly likely to be sympathetic when you explain.

Lots of self-defence books and manuals suggest you should run if you think an attack is imminent. That is fine if you are young and fit. But for those of us who cannot remember when we last did the 100 yards dash and are exhausted for hours if we have to sprint for a bus, it is pretty pointless advice, unless you know there is some haven of safety pretty close. And, in general, women's clothes and shoes are not as suited to quick getaways as men's. My guess is that nine times out of ten a woman would do better to rely on her wits than her legs to get her out of trouble. So do not forget that drink, or drugs, will slow down your reactions and fuddle your brain.

There are times when none of the above advice might be of any help. So should you turn and fight? There is no easy answer. Since many rape attacks are violent and often carried out with knives, bottles or sheer brute force, kicking and screaming can often make things worse for the victim.

On the other hand, there is no point in meekly submitting if a knee in the groin will give you a chance to get away. Only you can decide. One point worth mentioning is that women rarely punch effectively – slapping or pushing your attacker hard under the chin with the butt of your hand is probably better.

## Rape

There are still a lot of myths about rape. The stereotyped rape victim is a bra-less hussy, attacked in a dark alley by a stranger she gave the eye to in a pub. In fact, according to statistics collected by the London Rape Crisis Centre, only 46 per cent of women were raped by strangers and only 22 per cent were raped in the street, a park or woods.

In other words, more than half the women had had some prior contact with the man who raped them: either they knew him slightly; or he was someone they had dealt with through his work – a milkman, gasman, etc.; or he was a friend, relative, ex-lover or husband.

Almost one in three of the rapes took place in the woman's own home and almost one in five in the attacker's home.

Experts also say that it is a myth that rape is a *sexual* crime brought on by uncontrollable male sexual urges, or that rape only happens to 'bad' women. To begin with, the sexual attractiveness of the victim has little to do with it. Women of all ages, from young girls to grannies, are raped, and their backgrounds and lifestyles vary just as much as their age.

The Rape Counselling and Research Project say this: 'Rape is committed by men on women and girls because it is the ultimate, and most powerful expression of their wish to dominate, degrade and humiliate. Rape is an act of violence.'

So what should you do if you are raped? Go home, have a bath and try to forget about it? Go to the police?

Over the past five or six years a number of rape crisis centres have opened throughout Great Britain. The RCCs are charities, largely run by volunteers and can be found, for example, in Bristol, Nottingham, Glasgow, Leeds, Manchester, Liverpool and Belfast. There is also a 24-hour phone line at the London Rape Crisis Centre (01-837 1600). Their service is both free and confidential and they offer both immediate and continuing advice and support to rape victims. They can tell you about police procedures, court and legal matters, where to go to get a VD check-up or abortion advice. They can also find another woman to come with you to give support at a police station, a clinic or a court hearing.

According to the London Rape Crisis Centre, only one in four of the women who contact them chooses to report to the police. They say:

> The decision on whether or not to report to the police is a very difficult one for a woman to make. Many factors influence her decision.
>
> She may be too upset by the attack to even think of it. She may be clear that she doesn't want to tell anyone, except in complete anonymity. She may be frightened of retaliation by the attacker, his family or friends.
>
> She may be anxious about what will happen when she goes to the police station. Many women know they are unlikely to be believed. Others are justifiably angry and see reporting as a way of naming the crime committed against them and ensuring the attacker is punished. Many women see reporting as a way of protecting other women from a similar attack. We support a woman, whatever her decision.

If you DO decide to report the rape to the police:

—do so as soon as possible,
—do not wash or change in case you destroy any evidence,
—do not have a drink or take drugs to calm yourself down,
—tell someone what has happened as soon as possible so you have
   a witness to your state of distress and to your complaint,

—make notes about what happened, times and descriptions so that
making your statement will be easier.

Even if you decide NOT to report the rape, try to talk about it
to a friend. See a doctor to check for VD, pregnancy or injuries.

Under the Sex Offences Amendment Act of 1976, rape victims
are guaranteed anonymity. Until then, many women chose not to
drag through the courts with all the publicity that goes with rape
cases.

The Act was also supposed to make things easier for a woman
by limiting the circumstances in which she could be cross-
examined in court about her sexual reputation or experience. In
practice, the Act seems to have had little impact. And this is
probably because reporting a rape can still almost be as upsetting
as the rape itself.

LRCC reports:

> Going to the police is often a humiliating and difficult
> experience for women and we have had many contacts with
> women who have been very distressed and angered by the
> way in which they have been treated by the police.
>
> Women are not generally offered the chance to speak to a
> policewoman and are often not aware they have the right to
> request this. When women go to the police they are often
> met with contempt, disbelief and insinuations or direct
> accusations that they have provoked the rapist. Given these
> attitudes, it is not surprising that some women withdraw the
> charge as they feel too distressed to proceed.

And it is not surprising either, that the police persist in treating
reports of rape in the way they do. After all, their priority is to
establish the facts of the case to decide whether it is worth
prosecuting the man. They are not principally concerned with
helping the rape victim feel better.

They want to know whether you will stick to your story in the
face of the kind of cross examination you might get in court.
Sometimes it can be devastating to go through the ordeal of police
questioning, and the medical examination by a police doctor, only

to learn that the police have decided not to prosecute, because, in their view, the evidence is not strong enough.

That is where, once again, counsellors at a rape crisis centre can help you work through your feelings of anger, helplessness or whatever else you are still experiencing. And there is no doubt that the aftermath of rape can last a long time. Some of the women who contact rape crisis centres for help do so months, even years after the attack. LRCC say: 'A woman may think she should "be over it by now" and be urged by family and friends to forget about the rape. We encourage women to share the feelings they actually have, rather than the feelings imposed on them by other people.'

## Burglary

Although not as traumatic as rape or sexual assault, a burglary can also make a woman feel as though she has, in some way, been violated. The thought of a stranger breaking in to her home and creating havoc, rummaging through her possessions, can be extremely distressing, even if insurance will cover any loss or damage and nothing of sentimental value is taken.

You can spend a small fortune on locks and alarms and still become a target for the housebreaker; in one block of flats in London thieves used a chain saw to cut their way through front doors! But although you might not be able to deter the professional you can steps to persuade the casual intruder to find an easier mark.

To start with, there is no need to advertise the fact that you are a single woman. If you have a phone, make sure your listing in the phone book simply gives your initial and your surname.

If you live alone – or even if you share with other women – it might be an idea to change all the locks when you move in. Who knows how many spare keys have been cut over the years, and who has them now?

Do not leave a spare key under the mat, a flowerpot or in any other clever hideyhole for the days when you get locked out or lose your keys. A burglar is just as capable of finding it as you are. It is far better to leave a spare key with a friend or neighbour you can trust. Or keep a note handy of a local emergency locksmith (you will find one in the Yellow Pages).

Fit window locks and use them at night and when you go out. Lock up your doors at night, too, and do not forget to remove the key if you have a largish letterbox or catflap in the door. One day when I locked myself out I discovered I could put my arm through the back-door catflap and turn the key on the inside. Then I realized, if I could do it, so could anyone . . .

Many break-ins are carried out by youngsters who can squeeze through tiny windows. So do not forget the bathroom and the loo when you are checking that all is secure.

To check late-night callers – or callers at any time when you are alone and not expecting anyone – consider fitting a chain and spyhole. An outside light is also a good idea. Do not open the door if you do not know the caller. Even when officials like gas and electricity men call to read the meter, ask for identification. Do not employ odd-job men – fellows who turn up on the doorstep and ask if you want your windows cleaned or garden weeded – without checking up on them with neighbours first. If in doubt, turn down the offer.

Most people remember to cancel the milk and the papers when they go away. But the free sheets and the post can still be left sticking out of your letterbox advertising the fact that your home is empty. It pays to cultivate your neighbours – they can keep an eye on your place when you are away, and you can return the favour for them when they take their holidays.

Contrary to popular opinion, most break-ins occur during the daytime, but you might think it worth spending the money on a time-switch which will turn your lights, TV or other electrical appliances off and on while you are out of the house.

Burglars tend to be opportunists – so do not leave ladders lying around outside. And do not tempt them. You may think net curtains are fussy or old-fashioned, but at least they hide the hi-fi or the portable TV from the prying eyes of passers-by. If you really cannot bear nets then invest in some cane blinds. Or make sure it looks as if you have nothing worth stealing.

Crime Prevention Officers at your local police station will be happy to advise you how to make your home safe. Just phone or call in and ask to speak to one.

It is bad enough being a burglary victim: it is even more frightening to encounter the intruder. If you arrive home and find signs that you have been burgled – an open door, a broken window – do not walk in. Phone the police from a call box or a neighbour's house. There is a chance the intruder is still inside. If you go in he may panic – and you may get hurt.

Similarly it is best to avoid confrontation if you wake up and think you hear a noise downstairs. It is better to be robbed than raped or beaten up. If you have a phone in your bedroom call the police – but remember that other extensions may ding or click and give a warning of what you are doing.

Some experts suggest you grab something heavy – not to hit the intruder with, but to smash your bedroom window and yell for help if he comes into your room. Other suggestions include:

—Turning on your light– that way you will be able to identify
    him. And he may take this as a signal to leave.
—Locking yourself in.
—Pretending to be asleep until he approaches the bed then
    jumping out and yelling loudly.

The last option is supposed to panic the intruder and either give you a chance of getting away or simply make him run off.

If, despite all your precautions, you are still the victim of personal crime – whether your home is burgled or whether you are mugged in the street – you can turn to an organization other than the police for help and support.

The first Victims' Support Scheme was set up in Britain ten years ago and there are now 190 individual schemes up and down the country. When you report the crime to the police ask if there is one in your area. If the police do not know, check with the National Association of Victims' Support Schemes in London.

If you ask for help, a volunteer from the local scheme will get in touch with you either in person or by phone or letter. They will offer whatever help or advice you need – whether it is emotional support to get over the shock; information about insurance claims;

details on how to find out about criminal injuries compensation in cases involving violent crime; or any other practical aid.

## Useful addresses/phone numbers

Martial Arts Commission:   Broadway House, 15-16 Deptford Broadway, London SE8 4PE, 01-691 3433.

London Rape Crisis Centre:   01-837 1600 (24-hour line). 01-278 3956 (office).

National Association of Victims' Support Schemes:   34 Electric Lane, Brixton, London SW9 8JT, 01-737 2010.

## Useful reading

*Rape and Fighting Back*, published by the London Rape Crisis Centre, PO Box 69, London WC1X 9NJ.
Eddie McGee and David Lowen, *Fighting Back*, Sphere.
Syd Hoare, *Teach Yourself Self Defence*, Hodder and Stoughton Educational.

# Index

abortion, 126-30
  cost of, 128
  dilation and curettage
    (D and C), 129
  late, 129
  risks of, 130
  vacuum aspiration, 129
Abortion Act 1967, 127
adoption, 130-32
alcohol, 168-69
Alfred Marks Bureau, survey of, 45
artificial insemination by donor
  (AID), 139-40

banks, 112-15
barrier methods, 61
breasts, checking, 164
Brook Advisory Centre, 55
Brown, Helen Gurley, 7
building societies, 112-15
burglary, 184-87

cancer, cervical, 163, 164
car accidents, 89-90
careers offices, 34-5
cervical screening, 162, 163
child benefit, 136
childminders, 42
Citizens' Advice Bureau, 99

codes of practice, 98
*Cohabitation Guide, The*, 142
communes, 28
Consumer Credit Act, 104
consumer groups, 100
Consumer Protection
  Department, 99
contact clubs, 79
contraceptive advice from GPs,
  57-9
contract of employment, 37-8
crèches and nurseries, 41
credit, 103-105
credit cards, bank, 116
  store, 116, 117

dating agencies, 77-9
de Beauvoir, Simone, 7
decorating your home, 30-1
Delvin, Dr David, 52
dental treatment, free, during
  pregnancy, 134
dieting, 170
*Divorce and Your Children*, 142
driving, and the law, 88

Environmental Health
  Department, 99
Equal Opportunities Commission,
  36, 41, 46, 103

Equal Pay Act, 38
exercise, 172-74

family income supplement, 137
Family Planning Clinics, 55
*Fat is a Feminist Issue*, 170
flat-sharing, 19-21
furnishing your home, 30-1

general practitioner, choosing or
    changing, 159
Gingerbread, 142, 143
*Going Solo*, 142
gonorrhoea, 65
guarantees, 100

healthy eating, 171
herpes, genital, 65
holiday insurance, 153
holiday, activity, 151
    adventure, 150
    Gingerbread, 151
    package, 149-50
    villa party, 149
housing associations, 19
housing, council, 17
Housing (Homeless Persons) Act
    1977, 17

intra-uterine device (IUD), 60-1
    morning-after, 63

job sharing, 43-4
Jobcentres, 35

Kitzinger, Sheila, 52

legal aid, 87
legal rights, 90-2
lice, pubic, and scabies, 65-6

*Living Together*, 142
lonely hearts advertisements, 80-1

marriage bureaux, 82
Marriage Guidance Council, 55
marital arts, 177
Masters and Johnson techniques, 56
maternity allowance, 133
maternity grant, 133
maternity leave and pay, 39-41
Meet-a-Mum Association
    (MAMA), 141
mortgages, 24-7
    capital repayment, 25
    endowment, 25-6

nannies and mother's helps, 42-3
National Insurance contributions,
    111
National Savings Bank, 112
non-specific urethritis (NSU), 65
Nexus, 81

obscene phone calls, 93-4
one-parent benefit, 136
Orbach, Susie, 170
ovulation, 138

part-time work, 43
physical check-ups, 161
Pill, the, 49, 50, 59-60
    morning-after, 63
Portia Trust North, 107
Pregnancy Advisory Service, 57
pregnancy, myths about, 57
pregnancy testing, 124-26
prescriptions, free, during
    pregnancy, 134
Professional and Executive
    Recruitment (PER), 35

rape, 181-84
recruitment agencies, private, 35
Rent Acts, the, 21
renting accommodation, 19

'safe' period, the, 61-2
sale goods, 100
Sale of Goods Act 1979, 96, 97, 101
saving your money, 120-22
self-defence, 177-181
services, complaints about, 101-102
Sex Discrimination Act, 35, 36, 103
sexual harassment at work, 44-7
sexual intercourse, first experience
    of, 50
    help for problems with, 54-7
    under-age, 51
sexually transmitted diseases, 51,
    63-66
shoplifting, 105-108
short-life housing groups, 30
small claims court, 102, 103
smoking, 165-68
solicitor, choosing a, 85
squats, 29
state benefits, 119-20

sterilization, 62, 143-44
student grants, 117-19
supplementary benefit, 134-36
syphilis, 64

tax, 109-112
tenancy, fixed term, 22
    periodic, 22
    regulated, 22-4
    shorthold, 22-3
thrush, 64
Trading Standards department, 99
Training Opportunities Scheme
    (TOPS), 35
travel tips, 155-57
trichomonas, 64

vaccinations, holiday, 154

'well woman' clinics, 161
will, making a, 86
*Woman* magazine survey by, 49, 50
*Women's Experience of Sex*, 52
Women's National Cancer
    Control Campaign, 163
*Working Women*, 38

# THE WORKING
# WOMAN'S GUIDE

## LIZ HODGKINSON

Today the working woman is rarely simply filling a gap between school and marriage; but many women are still finding themselves judged in this light and don't know where to turn for advice on career planning, training, and guidance on equal opportunities and how to be taken seriously in the promotion stakes. Here is all the advice needed on these and many other topics.